COUPLES' COMMUNICATION HANDBOOK

Improve Your Communication Skills to Make Your Relationship Stronger

Nora Williams

Uranus Publishing

Copyright © 2021 by Nora Williams

All rights reserved.

ISBN 978-1-915218-16-2

This book is copyright protected, and it is only for personal use. You cannot amend, distribute, sell, use, quote, or paraphrase any part of this book's content without the author or publisher's consent. All pictures contained in this book come from the author's archive or copyright-free stock websites.

Disclaimer Notice:

Please note the information contained within this document is for educational and entertainment purposes only. All effort has been executed to present accurate, up-to-date, reliable, complete information. No warranties of any kind are declared or implied. Readers acknowledge that the author is not engaged in rendering legal, financial, medical or professional advice. The content within this book has been derived from various sources. Please consult a licensed professional before attempting any techniques outlined in this book.

By reading this document, the reader agrees that under no circumstances is the author responsible for any losses, direct or indirect, that are incurred due to the use of the information contained within this document, including, but not limited to, errors, omissions, or inaccuracies.

The trademarks used are without any consent, and the publication of the trademark is without permission or backing by the trademark owner. All trademarks and brands within this book are for clarifying purposes only and are owned by the owners themselves, not affiliated with this document.

Contents

Introduction	1
1. Understanding Couple Communication	5
2. Lack of Communication in a Relationship	25
3. Enhancing Your Communication Skills	41
4. Managing and Resolving Conflicts	73
5. Sharing Your Feelings With Your Spouse	99
6. Validating Emotions and Feelings	120
Conclusion	131

Introduction

Communication is at the heart of building our romantic relationships.

Many people live in the misconception that communicating solely means talking with their partner. However, this idea can be tremendously misleading; only talking without discussing important issues, making any real connection, or expressing authentic feelings is not enough to make your relationship desirable to you. Genuine communication in an open, fulfilling way with your partner can foster your relationship so that you both grow.

Essentially, we define a relationship as the connection between two or more people. We adapt to the dynamics of our relations by communication because people do not approach each relationship with the same expectations. Communication allows us to understand and be understood by our relational partners. It is also through communication that we react when someone fails to satisfy those expectations.

In our lives, we experience many kinds of relationships, such as our family, our teachers, our friends, our colleagues, and our neighbors. An intimate relationship is a bit different from the others; it can be beautiful, heartwarming, and exciting, but it can also be problematic or stressful. It usually involves an emotional, intellectual, and/or sexual connection with another individual. Everyone has a different expectation of romantic relationships, so it's natural if your expectations differ from your partner's.

Most people are not educated about how to communicate. Communication is an essential skill, and without it, a person is in trouble in an intimate relationship. If partners are not able to a mutual act of speaking and listening, they can't achieve intimacy. On the contrary, if the partners develop their communication skills, they will be able to establish and maintain a loving, respectful relationship between two people who love each other. Communication is one of the most significant ingredients that make a good couple. It is what makes a relationship work.

In counseling practice, it is common to meet couples who look for an improvement in their communication skills. Inadequate communication can often break down due to various reasons, for instance, when we are feeling distant, or there's been a big quarrel. If you're experiencing trouble communicating with your loved one, it can be really helpful to seek support from a professional couples counselor. However, some sources can come quite handy and effective, helping you throughout the path.

This book is written to help you to deal with couples' communication issues more productively and positively. Here, you will find advice that can contribute to bringing back the love in a couple while restoring respect and love for each other. Through the proven techniques, you will enhance those useful communication skills to confront challenging conversations with your partner as well as with others. Once you learn the art of effective communication, dealing with arguments and resolving discussions will become a breeze.

Through effective communication, the chances of misunderstanding decrease substantially, and the relationship grows stronger when both partners fully understand each other.

Chapter One

Understanding Couple Communication

Even though it may seem easy to say what communication is about in general, for decades communication experts have struggled to reach any consensus about how to define it.

We do recognize numerous acceptable definitions of communication. Still, we feel it's essential to provide you with our explanation to better understand how we approach each chapter of the book. We do not intend to say that our definition of communication is the only one you should consider as valid. Yet, your understanding of the content in this book is dependent on your knowledge of the definition of communication, which in the present guide is the process of using symbols to exchange meaning. To help you get the concept better, let's check out two main communication models: linear and transactional.

The Linear Model argues that communication moves in just one direction and simply transmits a message from one source to another. Take Watching TV as an example; you are the receiver of the message from the TV show as the source of the message. To get a clearer picture, let's examine this model. The Sender first encodes a Message, then through a certain Channel being verbal or nonverbal communication, afterward sends it to a Receiver who decodes or, in other words, interprets the message. Anything that changes or interferes with the original encoded message is called Noise.

- A sender is someone who has the duty of encoding and sending a message to a receiver via a certain channel; in fact, the communication starts with the sender. For example, you are the sender of a message when you text someone, ask someone a question, or even when you wave to someone.
- A receiver is fundamentally the recipient of a message. Receivers must decode or interpret messages in ways that make sense for them. For instance, if you see your friend making eye contact, smiling, waving, and saying "hello" to you, you receive a message from them. When this occurs, what you do is decoding verbal and nonverbal communication in a meaningful way.
- A message is the unique meaning or content the sender hopes that the receiver understands. The message exchanged can be intentional or unintentional, written or spoken, verbal or non-verbal, or any combination of these. For example, as you walk

across the street, you may notice a friend coming towards you. Making eye contact, waving, smiling, and saying "hello," are all forms of a message that is intentional, spoken, verbal and non-verbal.

- A channel is the method used by the sender to deliver a message to a receiver. The most common channels used by humans are verbal and non-verbal communication. Verbal communication relies basically on language and involves speaking, writing, and sign language. Non-verbal communication, on the other hand, includes gestures, facial expressions, para-language, and touch. There are also mediated communication channels (such as television or the computer) that utilize both verbal and non-verbal communication.

- Whatever interfering with the sending or receiving of a message is called Noise. It is external (loud music from the upper floor) and internal (physical pain, anxiety, or nervousness about an upcoming exam). Both internal and external noises affect the communication exchange, making encoding and decoding messages more difficult. Noise is in every communication context, and consequently, no message is received exactly as a sender transmits it because noise alters it in one way or another.

Although this model is straightforward, there are criticisms about it. The theory assumes that communication only happens in one single direction. It also does not explain how context, or our personal experiences, may influence communication. Still, other experts support the notion that communication is actually a more complicated process, where sending and receiving messages occurs simultaneously between both participants.

The Transactional Model holds that participants in a communication act as senders and receivers at the same time, creating a form of reality via their interactions. Communication is not simply a one-way transmission of a message. The outcome of every communication exchange is always affected by the personal filters and experiences of the participants.

While both these models are excessively simplistic representations of communication, they show some of the complexities of defining and studying communication.

The Role of Communication in the Relationship

A Couple relationship consists of many different aspects, such as companionship (interest and concerns, sharing experiences, showing affection and appreciation), intimacy (emotional closeness, mutual support, honesty), sex life, making a decision about practical issues and cooperation as parents.

Open and sincere communication is an essential element of all these aspects of relationships. You might have different views, but if you know them and why your partner feels that way, you can often talk things over and reach an agreement. It can be useful to double-check your understanding of what your partner is saying. Misunderstandings can easily happen and can lead to hurt, confusion or anger.

One of the major obstacles in communicating is that most couples have a basic mistaken belief of the purpose of communication. Most people consider talking with a partner as a debate in which each presents a preconceived version of what is going on in the relationship.

The fault with this approach is the misconception that each partner can go into the conversation with the correct perception of reality. This is not possible because none of them has the necessary information to define the reality of what is going on between them. One goal of communication is to define what reality is.

Communication is basically the collaboration of two people as they share and explore all of their feelings, perceptions, and thoughts to reach an understanding of what is happening.

Communication in the Ten Stages of a Relationship

Knapp's Relational Development Model is a well-documented theory on the stages of a relationship and is the original idea of communication scholar Mark L. Knapp. In this model, Knapp divided the average couple's journey into two phases containing five stages. These ten stages of interaction can help us understand how relationships come together and come apart. During all these phases, communication plays a central role. Before analyzing this model of relationship development, we should keep the following points in mind: partners do not always experience the stages sequentially, some relationships do not go through all the stages, moving between stages is not always a conscious act, coming together and coming apart are not intrinsically good or bad.

The "Coming Together" Phase

- Initiating

The stages of a new relationship start when you meet someone for the first time. This initiation stage mostly involves impressions and appearance; that is to say, people size each other up and try to present themselves in a most favorable way. In a few seconds, we make our first impressions. Here is when we try to present our best selves. We carefully observe the other person to know them. Physical appearance plays a significant role. In this phase of the relationship, people work very hard to display themselves as acceptable and interesting. They tend to choose their words with caution, knowing that a single mistake (for example, asking someone about a sensitive topic) may ruin their chances to continue a conversation.

- Experimenting

It's when two persons try to reduce their uncertainty about each other and may begin to test and be tested. In the experimenting stage, people exchange information and often move from strangers to acquaintances. A basic exchange of information is normal as the experimenting stage begins. However, sometimes the experiment may not succeed. During the experimenting stage, if your attempts at information exchange with another person are met with hesitation or silence, you may interpret their lack of communication as a sign that you shouldn't pursue future interaction. Experimenting never ceases in established relationships. Small talk is common among committed couples when they tell about their day at the dinner table.

- Intensifying

In this stage, the relationship begins to intensify and becomes less formal. People will start to reveal their personal information and will analyze the impression on the other person. As we enter this phase, we imply that we would like to open up more about intimacy, and then we wait for a positive signal before we attempt more intimacy. Feelings start to develop, and there is excitement about being in the relationship. Steady progression is key in this stage to save face and avoid making ourselves overly vulnerable. Examining the changing boundaries between individuals can be tricky in this stage, which possibly leads to conflict or uncertainty about the relationship's future as new expectations arise. Successfully handling this increasing closeness can lead to relational integration.

- Integrating

In this honeymoon phase, both of you begin to dig a bit deeper to see what common interests and values you might have. In the integrating stage, two people's identities and personalities merge, and a sense of interdependence develops. You start to know the person better behind the attractive face and decide if this is the person you would want in your life. At this point, the two individuals start to define themselves as a couple and emphasize to themselves, and others, how much they have in common. Here, they are certain that they share similar attitudes, ideas and interests. This can be a really exciting phase as you know more about each other and discover how you relate. But it can also be disappointing when you realize this person isn't what you thought he or she might be.

Even when two people integrate, they are likely to maintain some sense of self by having their time with friends or family separately, balancing their needs for external connection and independence.

- Bonding

In this stage, a couple wants the world to know about their relationship and make it recognized, honoring their commitment legally. In the bonding stage, the couple announces the formal commitment in public rituals such as weddings, commitment ceremonies, and civil unions. We can say that the bonding ritual is arbitrary, and it can happen at any phase in a relationship. In fact, bonding rituals are often annulled later on or reversed for a relationship that doesn't work out, perhaps because there wasn't enough time spent in the experimenting or integrating stages.

However, bonding warrants its own stage because the symbolic act of bonding can substantially affect how two people communicate and perceive their relationship. For example, the formality of the bond can make the couple and those in their social network keep the relationship far from conflict or stress.

The "Coming Apart" Phase

As a relationship goes on, there will be misunderstandings and conflicts, and the so-called 'indefinite relationship' may stop persisting. As in coming together, there are five stages in coming apart.

- Differentiating

As people progress in a relationship, thinking individually rather than together occurs inevitably because of external pressures. They may begin developing hobbies or other pastimes. The relationship as a whole will start to fade, and the promised everlasting bond will be broken. The feeling of dislike is usually expressed by the partners while they are still committed to each other. Individual differences can cause a challenge at any stage in the relational interaction model; however, communicating these differences turns into a primary focus in the differentiating stage. Differentiating is the opposite of integrating, as *we/our* reverts back to *I/my*. People may go back to putting boundaries in their life like before the integrating of the current relationship, including possessions or other relations.

- Circumscribing

To circumscribe means to put a boundary around something or to draw a line around it, so in this stage, communication decreases, and certain subjects become restricted as individuals verbally close themselves off from each other. After differentiating, partners tend to reduce their conversations and set up boundaries in their communication. Often, people prefer never to communicate the topic to avoid arguments. They want to have their personal space and activities, and they want a room of their own. They may use sentences like "I don't want to talk about that anymore" or "You mind your business, and I'll mind my own." Passive-aggressive behavior and the demand-withdrawal conflict pattern are more frequent in this phase. Once we realize that an increase in boundaries and a decrease in communication have become a pattern, the relationship gradually declines towards stagnation.

- Stagnating

In the stagnating stage, the relationship may arrive at a standstill, as individuals technically wait for the relationship to end on its own. They tend to avoid outward communication may, but internal communication is usually frequent. As an individual's internal thoughts lead them to avoid communication, the relational conflict flaw of mindreading occurs. For instance, a person might think, "There's no use bringing this up over and over again because I know how he will react!" This stage can last in some relationships.

Short periods of stagnation might take place right after a failed exchange in the experimental stage, where you are possibly in a situation that is not easy to get out of, but the person is still there. While most people don't like to remain in this unpleasant stage, some prefer to do so in order to avoid the potential pain from termination; some may still hope to rekindle the spark that started the relationship in the beginning; on the other hand, some others do take pleasure leading their relational partner on.

- Avoiding

Moving to the avoiding stage, for some individuals, could be a way to put an end to the awkwardness that accompanies stagnation, as people signal that they want to close down the lines of communication. At this stage, the partners avoid any contact on purpose, and they start to be physically detached. Also, they restrict themselves from any form of communication to avoid any conversation or an argument. Communication can be very straightforward—"I don't want to talk to you anymore"—or less straightforward—"I have a meeting in a little while, so I can't talk for so long." The stagnation stage will lead both partners to avoid each other since it affects their fundamental functioning.

- Terminating

This stage, as the name suggests, is the final stage of coming apart. The relationship totally terminates. The partners take different paths and will move on. The terminating stage can occur shortly after initiation or after a ten- or twenty-year-old relationship. Causes of termination can come from outside circumstances, such as geographic separation or internal factors, like a change of basic values or personalities that lead to a weakening of the bond between partners. Termination exchanges are involved with some typical communicative elements and may begin with a summary message that recaps the relationship and provides a strong reason for the termination (e.g., "We have had some painful ups and downs over our three years together, but now I want to be free to discover who I am."). Finally, there is usually a space left for future communication (e.g., "I think we'd better not see each other for the next few months, but you can text me if you need to.").

As we have already discussed, relationships are dynamic, and they are always changing. These ten stages of relational development provide insight into the complicated processes that affect the relationships' formation and deterioration.

The Five Types Of Communication

Five basic communication types make a relationship start and last: verbal, non-verbal, visual, listening and emotional. From the moment you see someone to the moment speaking initiates, seconds of communication have already happened.

As we argued, communication, in the simplest form, is sending out and receiving a message. Sending out a message takes place in several ways. Once you understand and learn how to apply all these five types of communication, you will master coping with solid personal relationships.

- Verbal

As obvious as it seems, verbal communication is fundamentally using language in the form of sentences, phrases, and dialogues in general.

But in reality, it's beyond that. The words spoken can be misunderstood. However, there is a way to avoid misunderstanding: speaking and watching for clues of acceptance attentively; this way, you can use words in your sentences, phrases, and dialogues that seem to resonate more positively with the other person and leads to a positive communication experience. Positive communication leads to more enjoyable interactions that will help the relationship to move forward.

- Non-Verbal

This type of communication includes tone of voice, pauses, rate of speech, facial expressions and body language (i.e., crossed arms). Even walking away is a meaningful example of non-verbal communication. If you speak to someone and they react with a smile, you likely feel accepted and that things are going on. Conversely, if someone frowns in reaction to your words, you get this idea that someone disagrees with what you just said. Non-verbal signals impact the understanding of communication that is taking place between people in a relationship.

- Visual

"Seeing" someone or having your eyes set on someone is still considered a form of communication. The moment you see them, and they see you, visual communication begins. You see how they look, their clothes, the facial expression, their body position and type, and instantly think, "I like what I see," or "I don't fancy it." If you or the other person like what you see, then the communication takes the "the next step," and the second type of communication begins.

- Listening

The most important of all five communication types is undoubtedly listening.

People often tend to believe communication means only speaking and underestimate the role of listening.

Well, to understand the sentence above, take this example: have you ever said something like "my cat just died," and the other person answered, "that's good news"? Why would anyone say it is good news that your cat died? The reason is that they were not interested, and they were not listening to you. How did you feel after that? Do you think you would have received a better response if the person had listened attentively to your words? Certainly, the response would have been more appropriate, and this indicates the importance of listening. When you are interested in what the other person is saying and listen carefully, you probably go to the next step of communication, which is emotional.

- Emotional

Emotional communication is so important in relationships, so much so that even Facebook finally added five new reaction emojis to its 'Like' button. Using this new feature, a person can react with emotions to a post with more than just a 'like' button. Users can now express love, anger, sadness, happiness and amazement. Why has it become so important?

For the same reason that I mentioned with the example of the cat. The person in that example said, "that's good news," and you were certainly hurt that they reacted with inattentiveness. With these five emojis, people can react emotionally and more appropriately to messages that are posted. Considering the role of emotional communication can help build a better connection with your partner. By simply taking into account the emotional communication with your partner, you can pave the way to have a long-lasting and incredibly successful relationship that you had no idea even existed.

Different Types of Couples by Their Interactions

John Gottman, an influential couples psychologist, has conducted research on couples for over 40 years, resulting in the categorization of couples into five distinct types. He considers the first three types as relatively successful: *Conflict-Avoiding, Volatile* and *Validating.* The remaining two are seen as more problematic: *Hostile,* and most problematic and divorce-prone of them all, *Hostile-Detached.*

- Conflict Avoiders

Conflict avoiders believe that the fights are not worth it. Problems pop up? No worries, they let it go. The relationship is too valuable to ruin it with quarrels, and they prefer to spend their time focusing on the positive areas of the common ground instead. These couples avoid expressing what they need from one another and appreciate their relationship for being generally happy. They become concerned about the idea of making active requests from each other and think of mutuality and congruency as true elements of happiness. Conflict-avoiding couples are aware of where independent functioning overlaps with where negotiation and cooperation are required. They prefer to establish clear and well-delineated boundaries and appreciate independent functioning.

They maintain their individuality as a person with separate concerns. When mutual support is needed, they can get these areas worked out well. Nevertheless, they try to be emotionally muted and content with low-key "good enough" communication.

- Volatile Couples

The exact opposite of conflict avoiders is volatile couples who are highly emotional. Lots of ups and downs, but somehow they achieve their own balance. During an argument, they immediately begin to persuade each other, and they stick to it seriously. Their approach is characterized by a lot of laughter, shared amusement, and humor. They seem to be entertained and energized by a good debate, but they are not disrespectful and insulting. Volatile Couples do not consider separation value in their individual lives, and they share large, and even sometimes, messy areas of emotional and cognitive space.

- Validating Couples

Validating couples is a much more relaxed type of relationship, with many problems solving and good communication skills. These couples interact with ease and calm. They have an easy-going manner of dealing with each other and are somewhat expressive but mostly neutral. While expressing emotions, they seem to be intermediate between Conflict Avoiders and Volatile Couples. They value supporting and understanding their partner's point of view and are often empathetic about their partner's feelings.

If they have opposing ideas on an issue of concern, they're both capable of digging in and find a solution that can satisfy both of them. Ultimately, Validating Couples tend to have a softer approach to each other, and the overall mood is pleasant and positive.

- Hostile Couples

Hostile Couples dedicate much of their time to criticism and defensiveness, and empathy is clearly in an ongoing short supply. There are many "you always" and "you never" statements and whining in their daily communication. During the conflict, each partner reiterates their own perspective, with little understanding of just how stuck they are in being "right." As in the saying, you can be *right*, or you can be *married*.

Hostile Couples, however, tend to modulate their negativity and never let it get completely out of control. Despite their perpetual conflict, these couples are likely to remain together in their unhappy union, as if they are married more to their misery than to each other.

- Hostile-Detached Couples

These couples live their relationship in a mutually frustrating and lonely standoff with no clear winner, only a stalemate. Hostile-detached wives are typically inconsolable, as all aspects of trust have been eroded. They have the same tendency to fight and show disdain, criticism and defensiveness in each fight, just like Hostile Couples. But Hostile-Detached couples are very divorce-prone, where Hostile Couples typically are not.

So how are they different? While their husbands seek to withdraw, Hostile-Detached wives will *keep fighting* until both are entirely drained and unbalanced. Hostile Couples will regulate their conflict, where the Hostile-Detached will keep fighting until they are worn-out. Emotional abuse is a persistent pattern in the life of Hostile-detached couples.

Benefits of Effective Couples Communication

We, as professionals, emphasize all the time the importance of communication in any healthy relationship. But you still don't know how it affects your mood, your love for each other, and even your day-to-day stress levels.

All romantic relationships can flourish only with effective communication through which information is shared. Living together in any romantic partnership can only work out when there is an effective exchange of information between the two partners. It is not surprising that many relationships fail to last long due to a fragile foundation caused by poor communication. Therefore, effective communication is crucial for a successful relationship.

Besides, powerful listening plays a vital role in connecting partners together and strengthen intimacy. Like communication, listening is not either an innate skill but an ability that individuals must learn with effort. When we deal with our partners on a daily basis, we are often likely to talk only and not listen; this way, communication becomes meaningless. If we interrupt or talk without listening, we make it difficult to hear what our partner is saying, particularly when our thoughts, feelings and opinions are basically different.

Effective communication makes any romantic relationship sweeter, easier, and more pleasant for both parties involved. Any relationship that lacks effective communication may go through misunderstanding, frustration, unhappiness, fighting and can ultimately lead to the ending of romance.

For all these reasons, if you and your partner will improve your communication skills, here are the benefits:

- Avoiding misunderstandings and fights

When people with effective communication skills experience problems in their personal lives, they may become worried, anxious, or even irritable, but they can prevent the relationship from worsening. They can handle this situation because it is normal for them to discuss their personal problems with their partner and count on their emotional support.

Instead of seeing their partner as a problem to deal with, they look upon them as a source of strength and comfort. Effective communicators see their partners as part of the solution rather than the problem. Such a positive attitude reduces the chances of misunderstandings and friction.

- Arguing respectfully and productively

Since everyone is a unique individual with a unique background and character, reaching an agreement on everything is impossible. When disagreements emerge, it is normal for each person to be confident of the merit of his position and to try to persuade his partner that his/her truth is the appropriate one to stick with. And so, an argument ensues. People tend to consider arguments as harmful to the relationship; however, they are acceptable as long as both partners argue with good faith and respect. Such an argument does not turn into a power struggle or fight.

In a respectful argument, the couple obtains a lot from exchanging ideas since each partner is willing to work as a team, is open to learning from the other, and considers solving the problem as the primary goal. In a healthy relationship, partners are motivated enough towards resolving the issues because each person is sensitive to the other's needs, understands the importance of moving on and the danger of letting the problem aggravate. Furthermore, if the suggested solution is the fruit of a joint effort, partners are more willing to do their best to cooperate in bringing about the agreed-upon solution.

- Knowing when to talk and when to listen

Successful teamwork on a solution to any problem will not occur unless both partners have had their full say on the issue, and each person is confident that the other person understands his position. Effective communication leaves no room for interrupting, ignoring, insulting, yelling, or other negative behaviors during the discussion; that is, each partner takes turns for speaking and listening. While one speaks, the other listens attentively. This constructive mode of arguing provides each partner an opportunity to express themselves in full detail while also ensuring that everything is clearly understood.

- Resolving problems through discussion

Many people avoid bringing up a problem because they fear that an argument will evolve. As said before, there's nothing wrong with arguing. An argument is basically a verbal exchange between two people with differing views regarding a situation or distinct solutions to a problem. If both partners are effective communicators, the argument ends with a friendly mood, and respect increases after each argument. It is so for when a couple argues rationally, each partner learns something, for instance, the strengths and the weaknesses of their points of view.

If two people argue constructively, after the situation is calmed down, there are good chances that they will have resolved their conflict with mutual satisfaction. Even when they did not find a solution, at least they have come closer to an understanding of what is mutually agreeable.

- Fulfilling each partner's needs

Partners in a happy relationship look for pleasurable common interests as well as personal satisfaction and validation of their psychological needs. What are those needs? Neither partner can read the other person's mind; hence there is a need for constant communication and feedback on this subject.

Everyone has different needs and the way or frequency with which those needs must be fulfilled. Most of these needs, desires, or expectations that each person wants to have fulfilled in a relationship are not explicitly expressed, while only a few are discussed with the partner. What effective communicators get to reach is the ability to express these hidden needs and fulfilling them.

- Increasing trust

Love is the seed that grows into a plant as people also grow in a relationship with someone. The soil is the trust between them; it provides the seed with enough room to grow. If the seed is planted in fertile soil, it will burgeon. On the other hand, if the seed is planted in arid soil, it may grow some leaves, but it will wither and die. Finally, communication acts like water.

When you spend time with someone and open up to them, you enrich the soil and nurture the seed, helping it grow. When partners communicate effectively and honestly, there cannot be a lack of trust in a couple. By talking and getting everything cleared out, partners know where they stand and can build a trusting relationship.

Chapter Two

Lack of Communication in a Relationship

Poor communication in a relationship can endanger the existence of a relationship itself. The symptoms of communication failure can include feeling like nothing useful is being said, arguing continuously, feeling like the other is not listening and, of course, acting defensively.

All relationships face communication challenges every now and then. Still, to many couples, the lack of communication becomes the norm. That's why, in couples counseling, communication issues are the most common complaint. In my counseling practice, I regularly hear couples complaining that they talk either all of the time or never. Taken literally, we can be misled by both descriptions. Except for some rare situations, like after a fight, most couples talk because they have to get through the issues of daily life together - *"Are you paying the telephone bill, or it's on me?"* Obviously, talking about the little things of life is much different from discussing the more serious life issues together - *"Are you happy with me?"* When a partner points to the lack of communication, it's usually about the latter.

When partners tell me they never talk, I know it's not true. Technology has made it easier to avoid communicating for real; that is, texting and direct messaging have apparently rendered verbal communication less necessary. Recently, a couple told me they text each other while lying in bed together. Even those couples who believe that they talk, don't usually mean about vulnerable topics such as their relationship or themselves, but about life in general, like *"I ran into Mike at the supermarket today."*

Poor communication can happen to everyone, even couples in healthy relationships. We often forget to share some important details by mistake. It's not a big problem to get upset and stop communicating for a while; sometimes, taking a break is surprisingly useful and part of practicing effective communication skills.

Before getting to work on improving your communication skills, you should first identify the areas that need some work.

Recognizing Poor Couple Communication

Below I will point out some telling signs that show some serious communication issues that might be threatening to your relationship.

- Your conversations never go deep

Remember the times when you could stay on the telephone line with this person for hours, never running out of things to share, always commenting on anything and everything under the sun? Those days are gone by, and there exist some of the most superficial, absurd conversations instead. Conversations that look more like a polite chit-chat with the cashier at the grocery store when you're buying some snack are light and superficial, accompanied by an evident sense of uneasiness.

- You don't care about each other's day

"How was your day?" is a simple question you can ask your partner. Trust me! It can work wonders. It shows that you wholeheartedly care about the ins and outs of what they get up to when they're away from; it also serves to bring about a topic to talk about. If asking this basic question never comes along by neither of you, then there's a serious issue going on.

Both of you tend to talk more than to listen

It's in no way a bad thing to want to be heard, especially if you feel that all your partner does is to talk non-stop. Just hold on a second, maybe your partner feels the same way about you too, and that's the reason why the two of you just aren't close to make any progress. That is, you're both engaged in an ongoing push-and-pull battle. When partners are too busy pushing their own agenda in such a complicated situation, accomplishing anything seems almost impossible.

- You lose your temper very easily

If every question that your partner asks seems to bring out a negative, angry response and sounds silly in your head, perhaps you're holding some pretty deep hatred about the state of your relationship. Imagine painting an alley cat into a corner, one that hasn't been fed for some days and hasn't been sleeping well. The slightest thing would provoke that cat, of course. If you're in a state of constant anger, there's something wrong at the heart of your relationship. Of course, every couple sometimes fights because every individual is different, so it's just natural to disagree on certain issues.

- One or both of you keeps nagging

Nagging is absolutely a telling sign of poor communication in every relationship. If someone constantly finds their partner yelling at them or pointing out the same demands over and over again, they will not be able to communicate efficiently, and their partner will not take in the message they are trying to send either. Nagging is totally counterproductive to good communication; you can only put up with so much nonsense before it turns into your natural habit. Just don't let it become a pattern because it's going to make you feel old and sour inside.

- You don't consider talking worth it

Anger is followed by nagging, and nagging is followed by indifference. That is the most dangerous stage of a communication breakdown because the next step is likely a break*up*. Sincerely, if you have reached this level with your partner, it might be better to simply call it quits and move on. When you feel as you're being taken for granted, or worse, your existence is being neglected, all you want to do is retreat into your cave even without bothering. At this point, you're at the edge of breaking up. It's time to utilize your best communication skills or just give up.

- Assumptions about the other person's feelings go beyond control

You've been together for so long, and consequently, you feel like you know them from A to Z. But keep in mind that just because your partner has always reacted the same way to a matter, I don't mean that it's safe to take it for granted. Actually, a person's reaction to a specific thing can change frequently. Imagining that your partner is always reacting the same way based on past experiences and act accordingly is dangerous. You'd for sure want the benefit of the doubt when it came to your feelings, and it's essential in good communication that you both have the breathing room to take a break and grow.

- You both tend to avoid hot-button personal subjects

If there's anything you fear bringing up, worrying that it could trigger an argument or just generally bad feelings, that's perhaps the most obvious indicator that the two of you have some seriously unresolved issues that need working on. If that's the case, so you're not communicating well or, possibly, you are not communicating at all.

- You prefer to share your problems with a friend than your partner

When you find it easier to just go to somebody else to express your frustrations, that's a red flag of the relationship. In a relationship, people must be open about their feelings and be intimate enough to share their sadness or concerns. If it's not so, you should work on it by practicing it or, as a last resort, with a couples therapist's help.

- Your sex life is pretty much non-existent

The role of sexual connection and mutual desire for each other cannot be neglected in a healthy and happy relationship. However, if your emotional, as well as the mental connection, has been so destroyed that even your physical connection is starting to fade away, then not even sex can save the relationship, and it wanes as well.

Negative Communication Habits

In my counseling practice, I see couples communicate all day, and often I have to teach them how to put away their unhealthy communication habits. Communication in relationships is a difficult obstacle to overcome, but it is the fuel that makes a relationship thrive.

Renowned relationship expert John Gottman argues that there are four fatal communication habits that, if done often, will lead to the end of the relationship; he calls these the "Four Horsemen of the Apocalypse."

1. Criticism

Criticism signifies attacking one's personality or character rather than the behavior itself. "You are such a lazy person" is an example of criticism. Instead, using I statements like: "It upsets me when you don't help out around the house," targets your partner's problematic behavior without using criticism. Over time, consistent criticism will weaken your spouse, causing them to feel disrespected or unworthy. This habit will lead him to build thick emotional walls, totally disconnect from you, and provide a foundation for unfair fights. When you send a message through criticism, it is less likely to be heard as you desire. The antidote to this habit is using a "gentle start-up." It means that you are supposed to focus on expressing how you feel, the situation that triggered it first, and what you need. He recommends to avoid using the word 'you,' which can imply being aggressive. If you are noticing emotional walls in your marriage, here are the rights ways to break them down.

2. Defensiveness

Acting defensive is an effortless behavior to engage in while in conflict. The main problem with defensiveness is that once you engage in it, you naturally become what your partner is trying to tell you and start making excuses, blaming your partner, and not taking responsibility for your natural part in the conflict. This habit is a way to block the attack in such a way that it makes you feel less shameful and more protected. When I work with defensive couples, I see their fights spin off into different topics that can take the conflict to a whole new level. Instead of getting defensive, it is important to take complete responsibility for what you have done and said as a mature person.

3. Contempt

The fact is when you feel contempt for someone, and you are looking down on them. You see yourself superior, and you examine every mistake your spouse makes. You know you are contemptuous when you show blatant disrespect for your partner by doing things like sneering, rolling your eyes, or using "humor" to down your partner. What must be taken into consideration is building a culture of appreciation and sharing your needs and desires through the use of 'I' statements. For example, "I'm feeling lonely every time you're working until late in the evening. I'd like for us to have more quality time together."

4. Stone-walling

It happens when a person is leaving the conversation. Either they leave or give every possible sign to indicate that they have stopped listening and are not engaged anymore. This tends to happen when someone is excessively stressed in the conversation and starts to go completely silent. This is one of the most destructive behaviors a person can engage in. Simply put, stonewalling is when you become nonresponsive. When you stonewall regularly, you are pulling yourself out of the relationship instead of attempting to work on it. The antidote for stonewalling is for this person to take a short break to calm down. Once they are in a better state of mind, it is important to re-engage in the conversation in a healthy way.

Reasons Why Partners Don't Communicate

When partners complain about the lack of communication in their relationship, they generally mean there's no good communication at all. The reasons why the lack of communication exists between partners could be countless. However, there are some frequent reasons that cause problems in communication. One of the biggest of them is that not communicating becomes the norm instead of the transient response to a specific issue.

Here are some other causes of not communicating:

- We tend to avoid talking about specific topics such as sex, money, children, or any other situation that potentially brings about conflict. While this provides relief temporarily, the issue doesn't disappear; rather, it requires eventual accounting for when ignored. Avoidance usually can turn into a normal response and, consequently, a pattern in relationships for lots of couples. This one, actually, is a persistent pattern in relationships.

- Sometimes a partner needs so much attention and affirmation by the other. More interested in what they want to say, they hardly realize there is no space left for dialogue and the balance of mutual sharing disappears. The listening partner often acts as an audience, but as mutual sharing gradually vanishes, the reason to talk vanishes in consequence.

- We often say something the wrong way or in a manner that we regret later. Nonetheless, instead of repairing it, we just avoid it. If it's a delicate topic and can hurt someone's feelings, it's best to share your insights in a gentle manner.

- When we don't listen well nor hear what's being said. The closer we feel towards someone, the less likely we are to listen to them as carefully. It's called the closeness-communication bias, and, after a while, it can damage and even end relationships.

- We are too lazy to want to engage in conversation. We'd rather hang out with friends and stare at a TV instead of using our heads and hearts to connect with someone we say we love.

- When we don't like something or are mad at our partner, we respond with silence and choose to punish them with no communication at all. When you are upset over something they did, not speaking to your partner is never the right solution if you intend to solve that problem. Ignoring your partner will only cause more troubles in your relationship, and you will definitely sabotage yourself and your happiness.

- Being too exhausted to talk is a state that you may experience every now and then. If this happens, lovingly tell your mate that you'd like to chat about this later. And make sure that you're the one who brings the topic up again.

- It's hard to make conversation if you feel like you talk about the same subjects all the time. Some successful couples pick different areas of interest to remain informed on, so they can share what they've learned with their partners.

- Sometimes a couple has gone through a dreadful traumatic experience outside the realm of everyday life, so much so that it has influenced their ability to express themselves. Be it a painful loss of a loved one, a major injury caused by an accident or a spontaneous abortion, and they avoid talking about it to escape from bringing up the feelings attached. Until they feel like they can talk about the issue, however, talking about anything else can seem impossible.

• Often when a partner is hiding an important secret from the other, be it a financial problem, infidelity, self-doubts, fears, illness or even a new personal goal, total honesty and real communication hardly can occur.

• Sometimes we feel that we can't talk over some issues without making our partner upset, angry or hurt, so we preferably stay quiet. We need to immediately stop being mind-readers; that is to say, instead of creating an imaginary picture of the reactions of our partner, we must speak our minds, delve into the matter and share and solve the issues together.

• If we are discontented with an aspect of the relationship, sex for example, we try to cool off our frustration or anger by not communicating with our partner. Unresolved anger is naturally a possible motive for avoiding a conversation. If we're mad at someone we love, we only need to get it out, explain our emotions and move on; only then we can get back to normal again.

• Our relationship is more about the benefit and maintaining a specific lifestyle than love and intimacy, so why bother and talk about anything more profound than what primarily interests us?

• Actions that you disagree with can be conversation stoppers. Talk about your preferences, and try to find some balance through creating a way for you to get more out of what's going on.

It's needless to say that this list can go on endlessly; however, I hope that getting familiar with the reasons I mentioned will give you a general idea of what causes a lack of communication between partners. The reasons could be numerous, but the results are the same.

Most Common Couples Communication Mistakes

There are several negative forms of communication that you should be aware of. They can ruin the communication process, so make sure that you are avoiding them. Otherwise, as long as you are sticking with your old destructive behaviors, you and your partner surely will become more and more distanced and alienated from each other. Communication should bring both of you more intimacy. It should be used to overcome the barriers that keep you apart, not to build up walls between you.

During my counseling practice, I've observed ten communication patterns that can damage our emotional closeness in a relationship. By recognizing the most common mistakes couples make while communicating, you're already on the right path to build a stronger, happier relationship.

- Blaming through Universal Statements

Universal statements are sentences that are used to make generalizations about a person's character or behavior in a negative manner. Using expressions like "You always/never…", "You are the one who…", "Why didn't you…", "You're wrong/impossible/crazy …", results in defensiveness, disdain, mistrust, withholding, and plummeting intimacy.

These sentences are problematic in two different ways. First, the underlying message in the mind of the person who makes such generalizations is that the other partner can't be different from the image that they have created. Second, this approach can be counterproductive since it emphasizes "what is wrong" instead of "how to be better," resulting in disagreements and conflicts.

- "You" Language and Directives

Ineffective communication is generally characterized by the excessive use of sentences beginning with "you," such as "you are. .

.", "you need to. . .", "you have to. . .", "you should. . .", "you'd better…" and so on. We call directives those statements that either pass negative judgment or tend to be bossy. Most people dislike being judged or told what to do, and when we use "you" statements, plus directives, it easily arouses feelings of defensiveness and even resentment in the partner. Besides, this type of communication is problematic because it invites a "no" response, often resulting in disagreements and conflicts. In the third chapter, I will illustrate many effective ways of getting your point across clearly and without using "you" language and directives.

- Assuming that more communication is the solution

Much to your surprise, even too much communication exists. Have you ever argued or discussed your point so much that you begin to say whatever comes to your mind? It happens because you're talking just to hold your own in the conversation. This is when you know you're communicating too much. Sometimes it's better to keep things to yourself, and it doesn't necessarily signify hiding stuff from your partner. Instead, it means you choose your words carefully, and you solely say what needs to be said to resolve the issue. The last thing you would do is mess things up while still dealing with the current issue!

- Forgetting to paraphrase / restate

While listening to your partner, instead of just responding with minimal signs (like nodding or saying "uhm" or "yeah"), learn to paraphrase. For example, if they are telling you about a problem they had at the office, say, "So it sounds like you are upset because your supervisor didn't appreciate your management skills." Note that this type of communication not only immediately makes you a better listener, but it gives your partner the impression they are receiving real attention and understanding. This little technique becomes especially useful in an argument. When restating what your partner says, you can continue with, "Did I get it right?" It will prevent a lot of misunderstandings from happening. Most of us are inclined to project our feelings onto others. Paraphrasing and restating are useful tools to help us understand each other more deeply.

- Expecting your partner to be a mind-reader

As said before, you are not supposed to communicate too much, but you also shouldn't expect your partner to guess what you're thinking. If you're waiting for others to read your mind instead of expressing yourself, you will never have your equal part in the relationship. Instead of waiting to be decoded, you need to clearly say what you're feeling. This way, your partner will understand that these are only your emotions and thoughts, not something you're forcing on them.

- Focusing on the person, not on the issue

There are two fixed elements in communication: the person you relate to and the issue or behavior you are addressing. Effective communicators know how to distinguish the issue or the behavior from the person, and how to be soft on the person and tough on the issue. Ineffective communicators will do the contrary, in the sense that they literally "get personal" by being tough on the person, while minimizing the importance of the issue or the behavior. Treating the person toughly and the issue softly can easily trigger adverse reactions from people, who probably take what you're saying more personally, and feel angry or hurt in consequence. Note that being tough on the person and soft on the issue also involves the frequent use of "you" language.

- Giving in without holding your ground

Don't give up everything without expressing your opinions clearly regarding a problem, just for the sake of resolving it. Your partner can't always win, and you need to let your feelings out and get what you need from the relationship, as well. If you never speak your mind fearing to mess up, over time, you'll realize that you're actually holding a grudge against your partner and end up hating your partner because you're unhappy in the relationship.

- Parental or Childish Attitude

Beware of the ways that you may communicate from a parental or childish stance. Parental communications involve giving directions and dominating, being assertive and patronizing, acting critical and judgmental. On the other hand, childish communication involves submitting and deferring, looking for definition or direction, being humble or submissive, seeking criticism or approval. There is no place for these destructive attitudes of communicating in an equal relationship between two independent adults. The proper approach to follow is to be respectful towards yourself and your partner when you speak to each other.

- Not expressing your appreciation as needed

Without showing your partner you appreciate them, you can't generate a warm and loving atmosphere as a background to your relationship. Tell them, "you look awesome today," that "I loved the dinner you prepared," that "I appreciate that you picked up the kids from kindergarten." These little things may not look that important; in fact, many couples take them for granted. But amazingly enough, I recommend continually reminding your partner that you appreciate them. It's a win-win game!

- Invalidating feelings

Invalidation of feelings occurs when we minimize, ignore, or negatively judge a person's positive or negative emotions. For example, "Your worries are meaningless to me!" or "Your concerns are absolutely unfounded." When a person's positive feeling is invalidated, their positive attitude will probably diminish or disappear. As positive feelings wane, so does the quality of the relationship. On the other side, when a negative feeling is invalidated, the negativity will intensify and stick around as well. As negative feelings increase, the barrier between partners thickens. Being one of the most harmful behaviors one can do in romantic relationships, the invalidation of feelings can lead to the union's end.

- Not listening attentively

When somebody else is speaking, instead of listening to what they say, we are only waiting for our opportunity to talk. We do nothing other than finishing their sentences for them, jumping to conclusions, and continuing the conversations in our minds, separately from what the other person is actually saying. It is an extremely unhealthy attitude to have since any discussion, to be fair, should have at least two sides. When you already know what you want to say, you often think about *your own words* instead of listening to theirs being said.

Stop acting like this! Take a pause and try to genuinely shut down your inner monologue and focus wholeheartedly on the other person. Don't focus on the first few words your partner says; instead, listen to their whole statement, take a moment to absorb it, and then think about what you want to say in return. It may sound easy and effortless, but effective listening is actually a challenging skill to master, and undoubtedly takes time and practice. Communication with your partner is based on self-awareness and clarity of mind. Give yourself some time to reflect on how you talk to your loved one.

Ask yourself, "Do I use gentle and loving words?" and "Do I *really* listen to my partner?". The good thing is to err is human, just make sure that you acknowledge them and try to improve yourself and your skills each time. It's not an easy process, but remember that the results will be hugely rewarding.

Chapter Three

Enhancing Your Communication Skills

So far, we have argued about what communication in a relationship refers to, how it functions between partners and its role in a couple's happiness. Then, we analyzed unhealthy habits and common mistakes that make effective communication between two partners difficult or even impossible to happen. In this chapter, we will discuss solutions and learn how to improve our communication skills from a theoric point of view, through explanations, practical examples, exercises and proven techniques towards reaching the goal.

Positive Communication Habits

The biggest mistaken belief in communication is that it is the same as talking or having a conversation. Communication in relationships fundamentally is about connecting and using your verbal, written and physical skills to convey the concept and satisfy your partner's needs. Some positive communication habits can help you out in reaching an emotional connection.

- Define your communication

Before you start improving communication skills in a relationship, you need to understand that not everyone has the same communication preferences. Some people simply prefer to talk, some prefer to touch, and others are more visual or respond better to gift-giving than a frank discussion of feelings. You probably know somehow which communication style works best for you, but have you thought about your partner and their preferences?

Communication and relationships are all different. Effective communication with your partner will result in recognizing this. Your partner might be telling you precisely what they need, but you have to be familiar with how they pass on this information to you. If there's miscommunication, you'll definitely lose the chance of building confidence and intimacy. Consequently, you'll both end up feeling disappointed and dissatisfied.

When striving to know your partner better, try watching how they respond to different perceptual cues for a few days. Does he or she respond most to watching and seeing?, Talking and hearing?, Or touching and doing? For instance, if your partner is more responsive to language, tone and auditory cues in general, making lots of eye contact and nice facial expressions may not be communicating as much to them as you imagine. You're certainly sending signals, but the problem is that they're not receiving them. On the other hand, if you discover to be an auditory person and your partner is a more kinesthetic type, know that saying "I love you" may not be enough. Instead, you must express your love with touch, and remember to do it often.

- Understand your partner's needs

According to well-known coach and speaker Tony Robbins, there are six essential psychological needs that all human beings have in common, but the order of these needs differs for each of us in accordance with our core values. All of us are moved by the desire to fulfill these six basic needs. Once you realize which needs are the most important to your partner, you'll know how to communicate with them to satisfy those needs.

These six core human needs are divided into the needs of the personality (certainty, variety, significance, love and connection) and needs of the spirit (growth and contribution)

Needs of the Personality

1. Certainty is the need that urges us to reach out for safety and predictability, avoiding pain, stress and emotional risks.

2. Variety is the need for surprise and excitement because relationships need healthy challenges that allow partners to grow together.

These first two needs are related to each other through a paradox and should be balanced. If there is an imbalance, you will crave the fulfillment of the less satisfied need.

1. Significance is the need to feel unique, wanted and important.

2. Love is the need to feel connected with others. Effective communication in relationships gives us the satisfaction of knowing that we are loved and cherished.

There is a relation between significance and love/connection as well. If you spend too much time seeking out significance, you will experience difficulties finding deep intimate relationships that bring you love and connection.

Needs of the Spirit

The final two needs are referred to as *the needs of the spirit*, which provide the foundation for fulfillment and happiness.

1. Growth is the need for constant emotional, intellectual and spiritual development. In fact, our relationships become stale without constant growth.

2. Contribution is the need to give, share and contribute. Sharing enhances our feelings and deepens our experiences.

- Verify if your partner's needs are being satisfied

There is one sure way to see if your partner is having these six human needs met in your relationship: asking the right questions and then attentively listening to the answers. Reflect on what your partner tells you, and if you're not sure what they mean, then ask again by restating their point and making sure if you understand correctly. The key to communicating the right way in a relationship is often not in actual verbal communication at all. It's inherent in how we listen to our partner.

Your partner might be communicating the problem precisely, but if you're not listening well, you'll miss the point. Resist the urge of just waiting for your partner to finish what they're saying so you can jump into your turn. That is no way listening; it's only waiting to talk. Instead, listen with a calm and open mind and try to wholeheartedly hear what they are saying. It will help you communicate better and allow you to connect with your partner on an entirely new meaningful level.

- Be honest and direct

Being honest and direct absolutely must be at the top of your priority list. In a relationship, you should be naturally able to say what you mean; therefore, clarify your feelings and needs, and be straightforward. Evading conflict seems only apparently comfortable and safe, but walking away from an argument is just a temporary way to deal with a communication problem in progress, and should be considered merely to have a brief cooling-off period. When you are discordant with what your partner says, you should be able to trust that what you say will be heard and respected, and so does your partner.

If one or both of you are against conflict, you may find yourselves repressing your emotions to please each other and avoid further problems. But beware that this temporary band-aid, helping peace to linger for a very short while, turns a two-way relationship into a one-way road, and that's not the sustainable outcome you might desire. Actually, the intimacy and happiness you used to share will gradually wane. Instead of ignoring issues, think of learning how to improve your communication skills to have a more gratifying rapport.

- Be Present in the Relationship

To build up communication in your relationship and understand what your partner is really telling you, you ought to be present one hundred percent. Your partner must entirely feel that they have your full attention and that they are your number one priority in life. It's difficult to listen and be totally present, aware and mindful when you're upset and angry or are working on things that may distract you from being wholly engaged in your relationship. That's the way it is, but it's essential to keep in mind that it should not become an excuse for neglecting communication with your partner. Remember that intimacy, love and trust are developed in hard times, not when your life is smooth sailing. If we gave up every time we ran into a problem, we would never go forward. Grab these opportunities to realize how to handle conflict and stress in a healthy manner, and enjoy watching your relationship grow and flourish.

- Try to Let things go

Don't let a simple talk about the present ongoing problem turn into a remembrance of all the bad things that have ever happened since the beginning of your relationship. In fact, this is the opposite of loving, caring and effective communication. Instead, evaluate the present situation and identify what you can do now. Take a pause, remember why you're both here, and remember that your goal, the outcome you desire, is to strengthen your relationship, build intimacy and trust, and ultimately learn how to be a better communicator. You can't just turn back time and rewrite the past, so let it go and move on.

Effective communication is more than knowing the right things to say. You should also be careful about your body language. You could give all the loving and caring words to your partner, but if your body language is not in line with your words - your arms are crossed over your chest accompanied by an angry face - your partner won't respond to you the way you desire. Communication in a relationship means being there earnestly, which signifies listening, loving and supporting with your whole being. Lean towards your partner while you listen to them, keep your face relaxed and open, touch them tenderly. Show them through your words, expressions and actions that you are their number one admirer even when in conflict.

- Break down negative patterns

You know about your partner's needs and are aware of their favored communication style, but there's still something notable that can affect your communication: how you're speaking to each other. Communication experts divide speaking manner specifically into four parts of pitch, pace, volume and timbre. The next time you're in the middle of an argument with your partner, be aware and make efforts to moderate these particular aspects of your voice.

An overly *high-pitched* voice potentially sounds defensive and immature. Also, if your sentence ends with a higher pitch, it sounds like a question; try to avoid this save for asking a question, or you might generate doubts in your partner.

By *pace*, we mean how fast you're speaking. Take a deep breath and slow down, especially when you disagree with your partner. To get your message across, speak calmly and clearly.

The second aspect to consider is *volume*. You should avoid competing to be heard. Remember that competition leads merely to shouting and miscommunication. Being louder doesn't mean that your partner will listen to your words more carefully; rather, it may cause the counter effect.

Timbre is basically your voice's emotional quality, attitude and tone. Beware of how you use your voice's emotional features and watch for red flag timbres like sarcasm or sharp ironies that can ruin communication in relationships and cause mistrust between partners.

When things go out of hand, change the pattern: try to be playful and use humor to keep the conversation flowing in the right path. Adding humor to the situation could somehow make it feel less severe and can bring in mind-blowing results for both of you. But why is that? The reason is that humor has the power of giving you back the missing rational perspective and balance; in fact, humor is an essential component of healthy communication in relationships. It also soothes stress and increases your physical happiness in your daily life.

The most considerable benefit of laughing in this context is that it reminds you that you love just spending your life with one another, even when problems show up. It reminds you that you're still able to enjoy your time together, even when life looks challenging.

When learning to be a better communicator in a relationship, it's essential to smash the pattern of hostility, hurt and retreat. For instance, when you find yourself raising your voice or being sharply sarcastic, change your tone immediately. If you're using "you" constantly and continue blaming your partner, switch to "I" and "me," or even better, "we." There's no point in dumping all your relationship's issues onto your partner. Breaking the pattern is a great way of giving the discussion a new perspective and bringing it back to where you can deal with what really counts. Communication is all about discovering what your partner's needs are, your needs, and ultimately, how you can both reach satisfaction in the relationship.

- Make a fresh start

At times, no matter how much you want improvements in your communication, arguments come along. This is when it's crucial to be aware of your negative patterns and make a fresh start before becoming more damaging.

Collaborative Communication

Everyone imagines that communication is simply talking and listening. Consequently, we fail to realize that communication involves certain skills that can be learned and developed rather than involving innate abilities. In my couples counseling experience, I've found the collaborative communication model very useful. It is a four-step process to describe how partners could improve their interaction in a more productive way.

Step 1: Going Towards a Conversation with Your Partner

The first rule to follow when starting a conversation with your partner is *Unilateral Disarmament*, meaning that you must shift your focus from your partner's words and behaviors to your own instead. Give up the need to be right! It's not a battle to win. However, this is not to imply that you are about to compromise and settle for less than what you really want in the relationship, nor this is to say that you can't be angry, disappointed or provoked. You do have the right to think all of your thoughts and feel all of your feelings. You must consider that your partner might have something important and interesting to say that is worth listening to. Remember that the conversation is not a battleground where you have to prove you are right to the world.

Step 2: Talking to Your Partner

During a conversation, there is only one single reality that a person can be sure of, and that is, you can only know about your thoughts, feelings and perceptions. You can be sure of nothing else, like the other person's thoughts, feelings or perceptions, and not even the reality of what is going on between the two of you. The only thing you and your partner need to bring to the conversation is something that each of you can be certain about: your own thoughts, feelings and perceptions. However, talking about yourself from your point of view might look easy, but it is more challenging than you imagine.

Focus on Yourself Instead

Although an unpleasant reality, you must know that one person is victimized by the other within almost all couples. The result is endless conversations in which the focus is on blaming each other. When you are making an effort to talk about yourself, avoid the temptation of lapsing into attacking, criticizing, accusing or blaming your partner. You are in the conversation to talk about YOU from your point of view, not about your partner or work or your friends or family or even kids. Take a pause and think of yourself for a moment. What would you say about yourself as a person and as a partner? Look at your partner and think of yourself. What would you reveal about yourself at this very moment?

Reveal those embarrassing or humiliating feelings

You must recognize your irrational feelings. Don't simply ignore them as inappropriate, immature, or meaningless; they are not so. Instead of dismissing or skipping your irrational or negative feelings, make an effort to talk about them. The feelings that you fear and oppress will cause you embarrassment or humiliation. What you must do is recognize them and talk about them with your partner. For instance, if you feel hurt or frustrated about something in the relationship, discuss those feelings with your loved one. Avoid the temptation of defending yourself by becoming victimized and righteous. This isn't about how you shouldn't be hurt or frustrated; it is just about the simple truth that you are hurt or frustrated and that it's giving you emotional pain.

Reveal your wants

We often feel embarrassed to talk about what we really want. Not the easy and material wants, such as I want to try that new Japanese restaurant, I want a new raincoat, I want to go on a trip, but the more personal psychological wants that are rooted deep down in you where you feel the most vulnerable: I want you to compliment me more often, I want you to be more affectionate with me, I want to have a baby with you.

Many of us have grown up feeling embarrassed about our wants. However, as you communicate your deep wants to your partner, you will be more in touch with yourself, and gradually, you will be a more authentic person, and your partner will feel closer to you.

When you communicate with your partner on this deeply personal level, many of the unimportant issues that always distracted you from focusing on the relationship will fade away.

Finally, talk to your partner with dignity and respect as you speak with anyone else

Most people have a particular way of communicating with their partners. What makes it particular is that it includes offensive behaviors such as being complaining, demanding, irritable, sarcastic, childish, parental, bossy … just to name a few.

While you are speaking with your partner, stop a second and ask yourself: "Would I use this way of talking to anyone else?" Do you hear yourself having these behaviors such as demanding (Get me a bottle of water!!), deferring (We will talk about the kids later!) or complaining (I'm so sick and tired of your friends!) towards other people?

Keep that in mind: Your partner deserves to be treated with the respect and courtesy you consider while treating others.

Step 3: Listening to Your Partner

Every conversation is unique and different from all the conversations you've had in the past, so don't get into a conversation thinking that you exactly know what your partner thinks and feels at that moment. You might think you do because you recognize an expression that they always get when they are angry or upset, but unless you listen to your partner carefully, you know almost nothing about the context and the situation.

Listening is a crucial skill that must be learned and developed. Just because we hear somebody talking does not mean that we are listening to them. Only when we listen with an absolute interest in understanding the person talking to us can we really get to know that person.

Listening is not about you

Listening is totally about the person you are listening to. So, put aside your thoughts, opinions, or reactions, because, at this moment, they are only irrelevant and inappropriate. The person talking is not looking for your advice or guidance. What they need is to be heard and to feel that you are emotionally and mentally present.

Hear them out

As you shift your focus from your ideas and thoughts to what your partner says to you, you are making yourself emotionally available by listening to them. While your partner is talking, put yourself in their shoes for a moment. Try to understand what your partner is experiencing. Empathize with them. Listen with your heart. When they relate an incident to you, try to feel how they felt in that situation.

Make a mindful effort to understand how they feel while talking with you. All you need to do is empathize with your partner on a deep emotional level.

Indicate that you are carefully hearing your partner

While your partner is talking to you, being a silent listener isn't enough; actually, you need to indicate that you are hearing them. During the conversation, try to be reflective, repeating what they are saying to you.

If your reflection is not close to what your partner means, they can correct you. You can then make adjustments until you have an accurate understanding of what your partner intends to communicate to you. Reflecting lets your partner know that they are being heard, which makes them feel understood by you.

Have compassion for your partner

When you listen to your partner with empathy and feel what they feel, you find yourself having compassion for them as a person. In other words, you feel your partner's human side, personal pain and emotional struggle.

You get a new perspective. When you really listen to your partner's issues, your over-reactions to them seem petty and unimportant. Suddenly giving advice or being judgmental seems patronizing and condescending. Acting victimized, on the other hand, seems self-indulgent and childish. From this perspective, you look at your partner as an autonomous individual you care about deeply as they deal with their own life issues, like everybody else.

Step 4: Determine Reality with Your Partner

After talking about yourself, provided that your partner truly listens, both of you come to a deeper understanding of what you are experiencing and feeling. Likewise, this happens when your partner talks and you wholeheartedly listen, and both of you reach a mutual understanding of their feelings and emotional state.

This whole new level of insight and understanding, accompanied by empathy and compassion, clarifies much of the ongoing confusion between the partners. The more in-depth awareness of each other's feelings does absolutely eliminate many of the misconceptions, misunderstanding and miscommunications that lead to this confusion. What remains is a sharper picture of the two of you and a new understanding of the reality of your relationship.

At this stage of the conversation, you and your partner possibly want to talk about what you have learned about yourselves, each other, as well as about your relationship. By discussing what you have grasped, you can identify the personal issues and reactions that create tension between you. Having things clarified, now you know what to look out for to avoid possible future troubles. If you get into trouble with each other again, you can immediately recognize what is happening and deal with it more easily and quickly.

Effective Communication Techniques for Couples

A relationship doesn't exist in a vacuum. It exists between two humans bringing with themselves their whole self, that is, their own past experiences, culture, history, emotions, and expectations. We must know that two different people have two different levels of communication skills when it comes to dealing with an issue. But fortunately, like any other skill, communication skills can be learned and developed.

One of the most common myths about communication in relationships is that you are automatically communicating while you are speaking. While talking to your partner is surely a form of communication, but if it's primarily about everyday topics such as

"How were your parents" "How was work today?" "How's your sister doing?"); obviously, you're not communicating about significant stuff. By communication, we mean the ability to convey the most vulnerable and crucial concepts in your relationship.

Communication can make or break a relationship. You can improve your communication and accordingly your relationship by putting into practice some of the tips below:

- Maintain a proper body language

The first effective technique is maintaining proper body language when engaged in a conversation. Body language, surprisingly enough, directly influences the way other people interpret your emotional state and plus that, it is vital for constructive, positive, and collaborative communication with your partner.

As far as we all know, no one wants to interact with negative people. Think about the people you dislike. They're usually unfriendly, overly aggressive, highly critical and most probably insensitive to others. While communicating, even if your words are friendly and kind, your body language counts for about half of what the other person perceives.

To maintain correct body language, firstly, you need to develop good eye contact. Good eye contact means that you look people in the eyes when they are talking to you or talking to them. Remember that keeping eye contact and staring are two totally different things. While keeping eye contact, take breaks to look away and give the other person some psychological breathing room.

Next, remember to express neutral, and ideally, positive emotions with your face as well as your arms and hands. When someone discusses an issue with you, expressing curiosity in your body language can indicate that you're interested in the person and the issue. For instance, keeping your brows furrowed and putting your hand under your chin are common indications that you're curious, concentrated and interested at the same time. While listening, try to avoid expressing negative emotions like panic, anger or shock. Instead, try to smile for mutually positive and constructive communication.

Finally, make sure that also your body is fully engaged in the conversation. For example, while talking, you can use hand gestures to explain your points better. Remember that your body should be parallel to the person you are talking to; this means that you must try to face them directly when talking or listening. Keep your body posture upright and relaxed and, most importantly, avoid crossing your arms, which may signify negative connotations such as defensiveness or feeling awkward and the like.

- Put yourself in your partner's shoes

When communicating with your significant other, it is crucial to keep in mind that the final goal of communication is to strengthen the bond between you. Try to put yourself in your partner's shoes and understand why they may feel that way. Do they have access to all the facts? Are they trying to get your attention? Whatever the reason, you must treat their feelings as of value and importance.

For example, your partner is extremely sad about not being invited to a social event that was important to them, and you may think this is a stupid reason to be that sad. If you think so, it's better to avoid expressing your thoughts and instead try to empathize with your partner like this: "I know the event was important to you but let's find out why we were not invited, so we can get the opportunity for the next similar events." It could never happen, but your partner will surely appreciate that a lot. In the end, it's these little things that count.

- Don't hit below the belt

Please watch your language. Remember that name-calling or bringing up an issue that had happened a long time ago and was resolved or forgiven will put effective communication in serious danger. Try to avoid the "you" language, which will surely take your conversation in a negative direction. Try calling your partner's first name with affection instead. This technique calms you down when you're angry and changes the tone of the conversation.

- Participate with sincerity

A conversation takes place between two people, and both partners should be active participants instead of only being silent listeners. The silent treatment is not permitted since the opposite of love is not hate but indifference. Don't be indifferent towards your partner. When your partner is talking to you, after listening attentively, respond without repressing or hiding yourself. Communication should be accompanied by honesty and transparency. Ask questions if you need to clarify some unclear points. If you are busy now, ask for a time when both of you can discuss the matter with tranquility and a peaceful mind. Another point to absolutely avoid is walking out the door without responding. Remember that you are in this relationship for a reason, and you need to resolve the issues by working together.

- Think before you speak, or you'll regret it later

As Napoleon Hill said, 'Think twice before you speak because your words and influence will plant the seed of either success or failure in the mind of another.' You may say something that can never be taken back. We've all had that moment when a series of words jumps out from your mouth, and the instant regret shows up through blushing and continuous apologies. If you could only think before you speak! It doesn't have to be like this, and with practice, such embarrassing situations can easily be nipped in the bud.

- Observe your partner

To your surprise, a fundamental way to communicate is to hear and observe what your partner is *not saying* through words. In a relationship, people get to learn each other's fears, weaknesses and strengths, goals, dreams, and values; thus, this knowledge can help both partners a lot in hearing things that can be heard through observing and not only talking. Some people are more comfortable with expressing themselves and consequently are better communicators, but on the other hand, some people are more introverted and tend to keep a low profile, so your job is to observe and understand them, especially their emotional and psychological needs and exigencies.

For example, Tina's husband, Jack, is a financial analyst. He had gained a few pounds, and Tina thought that he was becoming self-conscious about his looks. At first, she supposed that he wanted to lose weight and have a new look to be more attractive for her. Still, after noticing that he was looking for clothes online, she realized he wanted a new style because he thought his own was outdated and dull, and more importantly, put him at a competitive disadvantage at work with his colleagues. Tina understood that it had nothing to do with their relationship and, as a gift, decided to hire a stylist for Jack to solve his problem and make him happy.

- Ask open-ended questions

Open-ended questions are those questions that cannot be quickly answered with a direct yes or no. The importance of open-ended questions lies in the fact that most people often tend to hold back or filter their true feelings, thoughts and ideas. In a relationship, to develop deeper trust with your partner, you have to get inside their mind and guide them in revealing their true motives and desires to you. When you ask your significant other an open-ended question, while assuring them that they won't be judged or labeled, you can lead them to reveal more information about themselves to you.

For instance, your partner seems frustrated while dealing with a big issue at work. To help them out, you might need to ask an open-ended question such as, "what do you feel should be changed to make your situation better?" This type of question works wonders, in the sense that it will guide them towards finding a solution instead of being stuck on the problem.

When they answer, you can ask more open-ended questions to follow up, such as "what does it mean to you in particular?" This technique will help both of you dig deeper into the matter, find the fundamental causes of any problem, and think of a solution.

Asking open-ended questions will enable you to show respect, interest and care to your partner and open the way for both of you to build trust and communicate more effectively.

- Frame your views

Often when communicating with your partner, you may find out that both of you hold very different views on many subjects. After you've mastered understanding them by asking open-ended questions, you should have good knowledge about their mentality. That will permit you to frame your views in a way that is acceptable to them.

Of course, it doesn't mean that you should change your own attitudes to match your partner's. Instead, frame them in a way that is agreeable to the other person. For example, let's say your wife asks you what you think about her idea of the next family vacation. Let's say that you think the destination is not suitable for kids and has many negative features that she hadn't considered. Instead of saying, "I think this trip is terrible, and you are unable to decide," you need to frame your opinion in a way that is constructive to the dialogue. If you criticize her plan bitterly, she will probably be offended, defensive, and will become unable to accept any constructive feedback. In order to reframe your views excellently, you could tell your wife, "I can see what you were considering while making this plan, and from what you told me, I can see how it could be a nice vacation. However, I have some concerns about the destination based on what I read about it that I would like to share with you. Are you in?"

By framing your views to be acceptable to your wife, she sees you as a positive and collaborative husband rather than just bossy and critical. This way, your wife will likely agree to accept your feedback and take it with an open mind than if you had led with a harsh or critical statement.

Framing your views is an extremely powerful technique for engaging in open and honest communication without offending your significant other.

- Do not talk over each other

It may sound obvious, but when emotions are running high, each partner wants to get their point across, and a hidden power struggle shows up. It can signify that no one is truly interested in the conversation or reaching a resolution. Please don't interrupt each other, since constant interruption states that you don't think the other person has anything important or valuable to say and that you just want to prove your point. The reason behind having a dialogue is to hear each other's views on a specific matter. So, resist the urge to interrupt for the sake of your loving relationship.

How to Become a Better Listener

People are often convinced to be excellent listeners. However, when asked about it, many of them cannot summarize what their partner just said because there is an unconscious tendency to focus on our next points.

Two listening techniques can help you prevent that tendency; one is *active* listening, and the other is *reflective* listening. Both are relatively easy to apply if you're willing to slow down, stick to the present moment, and have the intention of giving space to your partner. For this to truly function, listening in a relationship needs to be practiced by both of you.

Active Listening

In this approach, the listener should be totally concentrated on what the speaker is saying to clearly understand their position. The objective is to make them feel safe to express themselves in case of having something important to discuss. There are three primary phases of active listening:

- *Comprehending* – The listener actively listens and analyzes what the speaker is saying without distraction or thinking about other topics.
- *Retaining* – The listener remembers what the speaker has said to grasp the speaker's full message. When it comes to active listening, everyone has their methods: some people may choose to take notes and others to use memory tricks.
- *Responding* – It is the act of providing both verbal and nonverbal feedback to the speaker, which indicates that the listener is hearing and understanding what the speaker has said.

The main goal of active listening is that the speaker needs to feel heard. To achieve this goal, listeners can use several techniques. Non-verbal signs used by an active listener might include smiles, head nods or appropriate eye contact. On the other hand, verbal signs used by an active listener may include statements such as "Mm-hmm," "I see," and any other statements that encourage the speaker to go on.

In fact, active listening is the right approach for allowing your partner to express themselves without any judgments or verdicts on your part, leading both of you to decide what action needs to be taken regarding a specific ongoing issue.

Reflective Listening

Reflective listening involves two fundamental steps: trying to understand a speaker's point, then offering back the point to them but in your own words. That shows you didn't just hear what the other person said but understood it as well. In the beginning, it may sound somehow strange and insincere. You may even think this might result in more annoying than useful. However, if you practice this technique until you master it, it works wonders to drive conversations forward. Finally, reflective listening is about getting to the heart of the misunderstanding and discovering what the other person intends.

Tips to Improve your Listening Skills

So far, we have argued about the essential role of effective listening in couples' communication. Here are five tips for becoming a better listener in your relationship.

1. Stay Focused

Focus on the main points that your partner is talking about. Give your loved one your full attention by making eye contact, and come to the conversation with a collaborative attitude, interest and curiosity. To reduce distractions, turn off the television, put down your smartphone and sit together. These little acts of respect indicate to your partner that you do value them and that you are entirely devoted to hearing them. When you're replying, repeating some of what they told you, using the same language, can be helpful. Attention to details demonstrates that you care a lot.

2. Adopt an Open Posture

To improve your listening skills, another essential point to consider is paying close attention to your body language. For example, it's believed that folding your arms, tapping your feet or pursuing your lips are all ways of showing disinterest, displeasure, or impatience. In contrast, effective listening can be demonstrated by a soft, open posture. Try to keep your body loose and consider leaning forward to show that you're enthusiastically taking in information. When the position of your body is relaxed, it conveys that you are open to listening.

3. Don't Interrupt with Your 'Solutions'

Have you ever finished your partner's sentence? Whether or not you've predicted correctly, you're tuning them out, which makes them reluctant to share their feelings and thoughts. You need to stop finishing their sentences for them and let them finish what they are saying. Everyone has their pace of thinking and speaking. If you think and speak fast, you have to match your partner's pace if they need more time to express themselves.

While you're listening to your partner who's talking about a problem, avoid suggesting solutions. Most people don't want advice unless they ask for it because they prefer to figure out their own solutions. Your partner needs you to listen and help them find a way. Somewhere down the line, if you come up with a brilliant solution, at least get the speaker's permission by asking, "Would you like to hear my opinion?"

4. Keep an Open Mind

When you listen to your partner, be careful about judging them or criticizing what they tell you, even if it alarms you. As soon as you indulge in a judgmental attitude, you spoil your effectiveness as a listener. Therefore, listen without jumping to conclusions, and remember that your partner is genuinely expressing their thoughts and feelings. It's only through listening that you will discover what's going inside their mind.

Don't take things personally. Perhaps, this is one of the most challenging parts of listening, since most people believe what the other person is saying is related to them. Consider that your partner is just communicating their personal experience, which may or may not have anything to do with you.

5. Pay Attention to What isn't Said: Non-verbal Hints

The major part of direct communication is probably non-verbal. We receive a great amount of information about each other without saying a word. Even over the phone, you can understand more about a person from their voice's cadence and tone than from their words. Seeing someone in person, you can notice enthusiasm, irritation, or boredom quickly through their body language, like the set of the mouth, the expression around the eyes, and the slope of the shoulders. These are clues you can't underestimate. When listening, remember that words communicate only a part of the message.

Couples Exercises for Improving Communication

Coping with delicate issues and sensitive matters can be a tiring task, but it's worth the efforts; learning and applying couples exercises for communication can surely strengthen your relationship. By improving your communication and listening skills through practice, you and your partner will enjoy a whole new level of understanding and appreciation towards each other. Therefore, I recommend these exercises either revitalize a troubled relationship or keep a connection in a happy one.

Effective Communication Exercises for Couples

If you think that your relationship is lacking effective communication, here are some exercises designed for couples. The goal of doing these exercises is to improve your communication and your relationship in the long run. Despite the targeted skillset (verbal, non-verbal, written), all exercises aim to build and rebuild connection and trust in the relationship.

- High and Low

This verbal communication activity permits individuals to express themselves without restrictions, while their partner practices attentive listening techniques. The most suitable time to do this activity is at dinner or bedtime. First, each partner must share the best part of their day, which is their 'high,' and the most disappointing part, which is their 'low.' As one partner is sharing, the other must follow active listening techniques to show empathy and understanding.

- Listening Without Words

This exercise focuses on verbal as well as nonverbal communication. A timer is set for three to five minutes, and one partner has the opportunity to verbalize what they are feeling and thinking without interruptions. Meanwhile, the other partner is allowed to use only non-verbal techniques to demonstrate understanding, empathy, and encouragement. When time's up, partners process the experience by discussing their feelings, observations, and ideas regarding the activity. Afterward, each partner will switch roles to have an opportunity to practice this helpful exercise.

- Reframe and Repair

Remember that sometimes in a relationship, a simple word or a reference to the past can make your partner feel insulted, criticized, or even devalue. Instead of ignoring such feelings, discuss them. Prepare a calm atmosphere and dedicate some time to bring up one hurtful statement or insult made by the other. Now it's time to work on the issue by talking about the cause and intent behind those words more peacefully and lovingly. This exercise provides a safe space for resolving past hurts that one or the other is still having a hard time getting over. In this process, the one who made the insult finds a chance to find a more polite way to express the anger, disappointment or hurt that they felt or may still feel while offering an honest apology for the pain they caused through their words.

- Eye See You

Sit together and try to make uninterrupted eye contact for about five minutes without talking. You are allowed to use non-verbal communication, but you shouldn't speak or make any noises until the time is up. Afterward, you can discuss what it was like for each of you, what went through your minds, and what you think the other was thinking, of course, based on non-verbal cues and how well you know your partner. If it helps, sit face to face and, if staring into each other's eyes, gets to be too much, play light music, lean your foreheads together and just enjoy this meditative silence and closeness.

- Role Reversal

Role reversal is an exercise that is usually practiced at communication workshops. In this exercise, the couples have to switch roles; that is, the wife becomes the husband and vice versa. Once they have switched their roles, they should adopt each other's habits, mannerisms, and speaking style; this way, couples understand their thoughts and motivations much better through seeing their habits from outside. When it is done, partners should start talking to each other in their new roles, meaning that the wife should talk to the husband in the same manner he generally talks to her and vice versa. That will help the partners to understand how the other person feels when their partner to them in a particular manner.

For example, if a wife yells at her husband when he does not complete his chores, then the husband can talk to her in the same manner. On the other hand, if the husband has the habit of criticizing his wife all the time, she should take up his mannerisms and dialogs to make him realize how she feels when he badgers her the whole day. This role reversal exercise has been working for many couples since they get to understand their flaws and make an effort to improve their behaviors. So, stay calm, be patient and positively take criticism.

- Send a Postcard

This is a communication exercise targeting written communication in which both partners are given a blank postcard with directions to write a message explaining a frustration, a desire or a feeling. Then, each partner is asked to 'mail' their postcard by giving it to each other without verbal communication. After that, partners are asked to send a second postcard to respond to their partner's message.

- Keep a journal and call it 'You and I'

Pick a notebook that you can both comfortably write in. Then, take turns writing messages to each other. You can use this notebook for random love notes, to express appreciation for something beautiful, or just to express a strong emotion about something without judging or blaming the other. Think about how the other person will feel when they read your words. Remember to express yourself in a way that won't provoke, alienate or put them on the defensive.

Assertive Communication Exercises for Couples

Assertiveness training lets individuals become aware of their most-used communication style and helps them develop a stronger and more assertive style.

Assertiveness training empowers couples by emphasizing the importance of communicating one's feelings, thoughts, and desires while being respectful to their partner's needs and wants.

Assertive communication increases respect, reinforces self-esteem, and allows both partners to feel valued and heard.

- Using I statements

A common communication drawback is when words like YOU, COULD and SHOULD are used during self-expression. These words cause a defensive reaction, while the individual feels blamed, criticized and attacked.

This particular exercise teaches couples how to eliminate these harmful words by showing the partners the right way of expressing themselves in an 'I statement' format:

One partner says, "I feel ____ when you ___ because _____. I would appreciate it a lot if you _____."

Then, the other partner is asked to respond to that statement with a similar format:

"You sound ____ because ____. Next time, I will _____ and I _____."

- Sticks and Stones

This assertiveness training exercise focuses on name-calling and self-esteem.

Each partner is required to independently list disrespectful and hurtful names that their partner has used towards them so far.

The couple then sits together, and each partner is allowed to read their list.

Then, each individual must explain how each term influenced their feelings of self-confidence and self-worth.

- Say It Again

This assertive communication activity asks partners to pinpoint three critical statements that were used during a past disagreement or an argument between them.

Afterward, the couple works together to reformat each statement to see other possible ways through which the message could have been conveyed without harsh criticism or attack.

Communication Exercises for Engaged Couples

Engaged couples should seek to strengthen their relationships with guidance and practice before marriage to avoid becoming another negative statistic. Therefore, communication exercises can be utilized as a part of premarital counseling with a mental health professional or can be practiced by the partners themselves.

These exercises are designed to make individuals aware of their own communication styles while teaching them healthier and useful patterns.

- Mirror, Mirror on the Wall

This particular exercise helps couples to practice verbal communication accompanied by active listening skills. In this exercise, one partner should tell a detailed story for about five minutes, and the other partner must reflect back what they heard.

The partner who is reflecting back is tested on their ability to employ active listening strategies, evaluate their level of understanding, and determine accuracy in mirroring back what was said.

- Future Goals

This activity assists partners in discovering and communicating mutual future goals and dreams with each other. Couples are encouraged to discuss short-term and long-term goals so that they can know what each partner needs to be happy and satisfied in the relationship.

- Music and Lyrics

This is a fun activity that utilizes songs as a medium of self-expression.

Each partner must pick three songs that they can relate to and then share the lyrics/words with their partner. This exercise is meant to prompt conversation about why songs are meaningful, the feelings evoked by those songs, and the reasons why a particular song was chosen.

- It's All in a Name

This activity is meant to develop a deeper connection, positive feelings, and gratitude between partners. Each individual is asked to choose a positive quality to define their partner for each letter of their partner's name.

Each individual is then asked to read their list while explaining the impact on their self-esteem and self-worth.

- Take Turns with a Timer

Sometimes, it helps to set time limits and give each person a chance to talk without interruptions. If it's your turn to listen, just listen and resist the temptation of giving explanations about something, or offering excuses for whatever you said or did that hurt or angered your partner. You can also take turns chatting about the great things about your day, which are your highs, and things that upset or hurt you, which are your lows.

Again, if it's your turn to listen, your job is understanding, support, and affection using non-verbal gestures — but wait until your partner's time is up. Between turns that can be regarded as a break, you can both thoughtfully process what is said by each of you. Both are allowed to speak during these breaks, but only to empathize and, if necessary, offer humble and heartfelt apologies. Afterward, you can either decide on an action to take to avoid repeating a tactless mistake or think of a decision to make for future improvements.

Chapter Four

Managing and Resolving Conflicts

Anyone who has been in a long-term or even short-term relationship knows that conflicts are unavoidable. They can happen for numerous reasons, but in general, it's because of some perceived inequity in the relationship. Couples often make all sorts of exchanges to keep the relationship equitable. We probably make certain personal sacrifices for the sake of our relationship and, perhaps, expect the same or similar sacrifices from our partner.

When partners feel that there is balance in the relationship, that is, the amount of what they give is equal to what they receive, being in such a relationship feels good. However, when one partner feels that they are giving more than receiving, the perceived imbalance becomes a concern for the shorted partner, and that becomes an obvious reason for a confrontation.

From this point of view, arguments can be somehow good for a relationship. They are the primary medium through which we can improve our relationship. If we're unsatisfied with something our partner does or doesn't do, only by confronting them can we allow ourselves to make our wants understood. Provided with that information, partners can then make the right adjustments in their relationship so that these needs can hopefully be fulfilled. Arguments also make partners come together to fix their problems as a team, and if they're successful at it, it will undoubtedly develop a stronger connection and make them feel more bonded to each other in the long run.

I know that it's not always easy to see the bright side of having arguments. It's no surprise that relationships may go through times when partners feel like they just can't get along anymore with each other. We might think that other couples don't argue as much or with such intensity, or they're just better at resolving their problems than we are. However, going through periods of conflict is normal. It happens to almost all couples, and we're probably no worse or better than others in this matter.

The surprising reality is that couples who don't have the least occasional arguments or little fights might have much bigger and more serious problems than those who have little arguments now and then. They may have serious trust issues or are emotionally disconnected; therefore, they keep their interactions at an extremely superficial level. Another reason is that they avoid facing their conflicts because they believe that their issues are unresolvable.

That's why they have given up, or their communication methods are probably so dysfunctional that even minor confrontations turn into uncontrollable major fights. Other couples, such as those who have traditional views of men and women's roles, may avoid particular issues because one or the other partner, or even both of them, are not willing to change or even discuss those issues.

Nevertheless, when a couple dismisses issues to avoid conflicts, any aspect of their relationship that causes frustration or discontent will remain unresolved. Consequently, an unhappy partner doesn't feel that they have the power or the means of improving the relationship. Now, the question arises: how do we know that there's too much fighting in our relationship? That depends thoroughly on partners and their tolerance for confrontation. More important than how often couples argue is how they behave when they do.

In particular, we're referring to partners' behavior towards each other in the heat of an argument. In large part, that determines whether or not our communication is effective, and by that, we mean it accomplishes the ultimate objectives of a problem, and we do it efficiently. We know we're efficient when our disagreements are not drawn out longer than necessary, when our ongoing problems don't move on to matters that have nothing to do with them, and when they don't go towards personal attacks or past resentments or disappointments. Lastly, we know we are efficient in our arguments when both of us feel better about each other, and the relationship after the argument has ended.

The Roots of Couples Conflicts

Poor communication skills, by and large, are the major causes of conflicts in relationships. By dealing with conflicts constructively, you can obtain a deeper understanding of your partner and find a proper solution that works for both of you. On the flip side, it's also possible that conflicts create and escalate ill will without resolving anything.

The first step towards reaching a greater understanding of the nature of the conflict, as well as a greater balance in the relationship, is to identify the reasons why a couple is drawn into an argument.

All of us are more or less familiar with the issues evoking tension and consequently conflict; those issues could be money, housework and family responsibilities, jealousy, education of children, the vision of the future as a couple, etc. Here, the principal question to answer is: what are the basic psychological mechanisms beneath the surface of arguments from which conflicts arise in a couple? I've spotted twelve. Let's have a brief look at them together.

1. Control and Dominance

Like animals, we have a strong desire for pecking order (defined as a sequence or hierarchy of authority), even within our intimate relationships. Wanting to have power over others is part of our human nature; actually, we enjoy feeling superior – it means we get what we want from the relationship. Though in practice, through this need for dominance, we are hurting the one we were meant to care about, more than anyone else. Instead of wanting to control your partner, try putting yourself in their shoes. Keep that in mind: intimidation drives away intimacy, while respect and empathy encourage it.

2. Blame

It's hard to give up the idea that it's always the other person to blame. In such situations, using a 'blame cost-benefit analysis' is recommended, which works like this: draw two columns on a piece of paper, one column is for the advantages of blaming the other person and the other for the disadvantages. Advantages might include: 'I should not feel guilty, I don't need to change, I can feel morally superior.' Disadvantages might be: 'I won't succeed in getting closer to my partner, I'll be stuck in a cycle, and nothing will change at all.' If the list of advantages is longer, you have most probably succumbed to blame as a strong motivation for conflict. If your list is more like fifty-fifty, it's certainly tempting to want the other person to shoulder half the blame. Yet, if you want to have a better relationship, you must concentrate, first and foremost, on changing yourself.

3. Self-blame

If we accept all the blame in our relationship, we are actually rewarded, in the sense that through giving in, we are preventing criticism from the other person. However, that takes a lot of mental energy, and consequently, we're not much fun to be around. Instead of self-blame and taking the whole responsibility of failures, think of sharing the responsibility for the things going wrong and take a neutral adult stance rather than an emotionally charged one. Remember that in a relationship, there are always two people communicating with each other and never one!

4. Narcissism

Although a little bit of self-absorption is acceptable, if we find ourselves getting angry at the slightest hint of criticism and losing our temper, we are succumbing to the captivating power of narcissism. To resolve such an issue, try a persuasive technique called 'the law of opposites': When you try to defend yourself against a criticism that is unfair or irrational, you instantly prove it to be valid. If you agree with it, then you prove it wrong.' For example, if your partner claims, 'you never listen to me' and you respond with, 'you may be right about that,' you are already proving that you are listening to them.

5. Revenge

So angry with her husband Paul, who stayed out late without telling her, Nora switched off her mobile, saying: 'I knew he'd worry if he couldn't get hold of me,' she says, 'and that was what I wanted.' It is easy to deeply dwell on what our partner has done to us while overlooking our provocative behavior; but, the temptation for revenge will finally ruin our desire and eventually the opportunity to have a loving relationship. As you might already know, revenge neither makes us happy nor gives us satisfaction; all it gives us is a momentary, false sense of righteousness. The most prolonged international conflicts have usually been fueled by revenge; in those conflicts, nobody wins, and nobody wants to declare a ceasefire, but at some point, for the good of the nations and the world, somebody has to break the cycle.

6. Justice and Fairness

If our partner doesn't meet our expectations, we feel that we have every right to punish them. In a heated discussion, how often do we hear ourselves say, 'It's not fair at all' when what we actually mean is, 'This isn't what I want'? This distorts what is going on, in the sense that it is reasoning informed merely based on how we feel, or an assumption that our feelings reflect the way things really are for our partner. It supports the erroneous idea that it is the other person who has to change and allows us to justify cruel and insensitive behavior towards our partner. The key is to realize that what we said doesn't have anything to do with fairness or justice. When we are vexed with our partner, we flood our minds with negative thoughts that may sound valid at that particular moment, yet, beware that those thoughts inevitably contain errors.

7. Competition

The desire to win is natural for everyone; however, this desire keeps the battle alive. After years of an unhappy, physically abusive relationship, Elisa finally found the strength to leave her husband, Philip – only to go back to him a week later. She said, "we were arguing on the phone, and he told me: 'I never thought you could be a quitter.' I went back to him only to prove him wrong." Again, she left Philip for a good eight months, and later they remarried. Their new relationship couldn't be more different. She believes that she's still competitive, but not in her relationship. "Now, I learned that my husband is my biggest fan; he is my other half, not my opponent at all."

8. Anger and bitterness

Anger can give us a sense of purpose, particularly if our relationship is draining our energy. It may be expressed in three distinct ways: *active aggression*, which means looking for a confrontation, *passive aggression* that is unproductively avoiding confrontation, and *respectfully sharing your anger* with your partner. The last one is the least practiced, but absolutely the most effective. To overcome anger, we need to work on our ability to listen. The 'one-minute drill,' which is a practical method, can undoubtedly help you. For about thirty seconds, calmly allow your partner to make their point, say nothing, only listen and make sure your body language is positive and open. Then, for the next thirty seconds, try to paraphrase what your partner said, but in a very accurate and respectful way.

9. Scapegoating

Calling our partner as defective or inferior has the advantage of giving us a clear, though inaccurate, explanation for all our relationship problems. Statements such as, 'You always do that' or, 'You're so silly' are easy to make but cause us to look for evidence to support our labeling. Sometimes, we reinforce it by repeating such statements to others, and as a hot gossip, it is a process we might even secretly enjoy. But, remember that there will always be evidence to support just the opposite statement. Seek out that evidence, and you will see the power of scapegoating. For instance, instead of saying, 'You're totally unreliable,' ask what evidence there is to support the opposite statement, 'You're very reliable.' It draws attention to their positive behavior and gives us a more balanced picture of their history. We might enjoy reminding them of their failings because it creates drama and makes us appear as the victim, but what about the times they supported and loved us? Think of that.

10. Pride and Shame

Being forced to look at our flaws, especially by someone we love, can feel painful, so instead, we build a wall and go into our defensive mode. The key to dealing with this is to rethink and even redefine what it means to be vulnerable. When you are completely vulnerable, you are invulnerable because you don't have anything to hide anymore; in other words, your vulnerability becomes your greatest strength. We should always keep in mind that we can reach truly deep intimacy with our partner only through facing our failings and shortcomings.

11. Truth

In a fight with your partner, the subtext is often 'I'm right, and you're wrong.' But what if both of you are right? Take this stance, and the majority of your conflicts are nipped in the bud. You might have heard that anything that anyone says has some truth in it. Try to seek out the truth instead of ignoring their views completely.

12. Hidden Agendas

Of the twelve causes of conflict, this is most difficult to confront. What is your hidden agenda? Do you settle for your relationship's flaws and shortcomings, because deep down you benefit from it? Jessica is the main breadwinner in her relationship and frequently works until 11 pm. Despite his often-expressed annoyance, her partner Chris is secretly content that he has his evenings to himself and can drink, eat or go out as he pleases. To your surprise, there are always rewards for the problems in your relationship, meaning that they aren't problems. It may be that you like things the way they actually are, yet, the price that you'd pay for not being honest is a lack of or even totally losing intimacy in your relationship. Admitting your hidden agenda is the first step in making that right.

Conflict Patterns that Damage Relationships

Believe it or not, every intimate relationship has its peaks and valleys. No matter how compatible the partners, they are bound to occasional disagreements. If those conflicts are trivial, the couple will eventually make up and let them go. On the other hand, if they are serious but remain unresolved, they can damage the relationship over time. The process upon which the couples rely to resolve disputes is their conflict patterns. These patterns not only reveal a lot about the relationship but also can predict its future.

Unfortunately, in my working experience with couples, I see partners reiterate the same negative outcomes, not learning from their repeated similar arguments. As couples begin to identify their own ineffective and damaging fighting patterns, they will be able to challenge and surely change them over time. There are many different examples of futile negative conflict patterns, but they all have the following characteristics in common. These conflict patterns are:

- Exaggerated and dramatic.
- Never resolve the dispute at hand.
- Likely to result in amnesia after they end.
- Dishonoring of vulnerability or sacred information.
- Blind to causing embarrassment or humiliation.
- Commonly infiltrated by frequent interruptions, invalidations, or repeated defensive responses.

The following are the three most common unhealthy patterns occurring in couples' discussions. Understanding these patterns and keeping them in mind can help you to be aware of what you are experiencing and to change your approach, and take new actions when they happen.

- Attack vs. Attack

This one is all about self-protection. Someone feels attacked, and naturally they counter-attack. It's about trying to prove that your partner is wrong and only you are right. Arguments can worsen until one of you disconnects.

The more this happens, the more we expect it. In fact, we plan our arguments ahead of time and get ready for them with the counterpunch. At this point, the desire to win becomes more important than the desire to be connected to your partner.

Amelia tells me about her experience as: 'I used to fall into this trap every time. All I wanted was to win the argument at all costs, but Mike and I both realized that we were losing the precious relationship we had created over the years, just because of some childish and stupid reasons'.

- Demand vs. Withdraw

This is probably the most widespread pattern. One partner makes a demand, which could even be a demand for more connection. The other partner protests the implied criticism by withdrawing. The withdrawal causes the demander to make more demands, which causes the withdrawer to pull away even more, and this goes on without an end.

We usually see this as the advice cycle. One partner desires an emotional connection, and the other replies with logical advice. It can be interpreted as not responding at all. The advice itself may be helpful, but it's given without recognizing the emotions. The partner who is giving advice thinks that he/she is helping, but the other partner doesn't feel an emotional connection. The result is more distance in the relationship, not connection at all.

- Withdraw vs. Withdraw

Laura had decided that it was better not to bring up things in her relationship with Robert to avoid future fights and quarrels. But the results were not as promising as they might have imagined; Robert withdrew and just didn't say anything. They still got along, and she thought it was great that they didn't ever fight. Still, the distance between them grew more and more.

When both people are withdrawing, it seems very peaceful. Eventually, resentments can build up. The relationship can turn into just being roommates with very little connection.

How to Argue in a Healthy Way

When it comes to relationships, conflict is unavoidable. But it doesn't necessarily have to be emotionally distressing or callous. We all know that couples can disagree and, yet, while arguing over a serious issue, they can still show compassion and respect for each other.

An interesting but sad fact is that married couples who experience *no* conflicts at all in their relationship are usually the ones whose marriages end in divorce. Relationships that can't be saved are those where the flame has totally gone out, or it wasn't there in the first place. When one or both partners are indifferent towards their relationship, they don't care enough to fight over their issues.

That said, I want to point out that frequent and heated fights are certainly not healthy or sustainable, either. You are allowed to have conflicts with your partner, but only in a constructive and productive way. I'd like to give you this good news that productive and respectful arguments can surprisingly bring you closer together more than you can imagine. In my counseling experience, I've observed that expressing anger to a romantic partner may cause short-term discomfort. Still, in the long run, it leads to honest conversations that benefited the relationship prominently.

If you're ready to navigate conflict with your partner more healthily and productively, keep these essential tips in mind during your next argument:

- Be curious about your fights

During counseling sessions, I often ask couples, 'What does the late afternoon fight look like on weekdays?' They kind of smile because they know that they have the same fight over and over without the slightest difference. It's like they always fight following a script, without going towards a solution. A common cause of the late afternoon fight is one partner needing to tell the other about their day, and the other partner not feeling like it — needing a minute to calm down and relax after work. That probably leads to one partner accusing the other of not caring enough about them, and the other feeling attacked.

Instead, I encourage couples to identify what exactly triggers this repetitive fight and try out ways to compromise instead of allowing the fight to break out. Rather than following the same old pattern, which has become like a script, notice that you fight when one partner gets home.

So, what you need to do is: suggest a new method to stick to. You can say: 'What if we pause now, say hello (or kiss hello), give it twenty minutes, and come back together?'. This way, both partners can imply that they are more than willing to hear about the other person's day, and together, find the best way to do that.

- Schedule a Time For Conflict

When you or your partner isn't feeling well because they are stressed, angry or sad, it cannot be the best time to bring up sort of heavy or challenging topics. When people do not feel comfortable or well, their emotions may make communication in relationships difficult or problematic because they might get easily annoyed, angry or are not completely focused on the issue. By picking the right time to talk about something, you will see that communication is more effective. If it is difficult for you to time this well, perhaps it is an idea to schedule a moment in the week for such conversations.

- Take Timeout if One of You Needs It

It's normal for one or both partners to enter 'fight, flight or freeze' mode during an argument. People enter one of these modes when they feel that they may be in danger. 'Fight or flight' refers to when stress hormones activate to give people more energy to either fight the stressor or run from the situation. And "freeze" mode happens when a person simply does not react at all, hoping that the stressor finally loses interest to continue the fight. When a couple is in this risky zone, problem-solving is highly improbable because they focus solely on reacting to the threat they feel from their partner. If only one partner is in the 'fight, flight or freeze mode,' while the other wants to resolve the issue, it can frustrate both people and worsen the fight.

If you're upset with your partner and they're trying to problem solve, it can feel like they're not even listening. I often recommend that one of the partners take a timeout in such situations. And you can frame the timeout in a way that doesn't give your partner the impression that you're avoiding the situation by walking away. Perhaps one partner says: 'Okay, I do want to have this conversation. I just need about ten minutes to cool off. I love you, and I want to assure you I'm not going anywhere. We will come back to this, and we'll figure it out together.' After the brief hiatus, both partners will certainly be in a better mental condition to make real progress with the discussion.

- Make Requests, NOT Complaints

Fights frequently start with these two words: 'You always.' Sometimes, people, rather than asking their partner to do something they'd like them to do, for example cleaning up around the house, they simply jump to make accusations. But I'm assuring you that this method will not work out. You're not going to get what you want because of the way you're asking for it. It's strangely easier for people to ask their partner why they never do something rather than making a request for doing it. They prefer using 'You never…'. I know! It's weird.

Saying, 'I'm not feeling great. I'm stressed out about the way the house looks. Would you mind picking up some stuff?' is more respectful and straightforward than putting your loved one down for his or her failure about satisfying your needs. Using this tip while in a similar situation, you'll see that your partner is more willing to start and complete the task.

- Listen without interrupting

When it comes to sitting down and resolving conflicts, as said before, it's crucial to listen without interrupting, although this can turn out more challenging than it actually seems. If your partner says that he/she doesn't feel heard, you must listen until your partner is finished speaking. Afterward, you can ask for clarification if there is something unclear. Asking 'what makes you think that I'm not listening?' is a much more tactful way to address your partner's complaint than simply saying, 'well, I am listening, so you must feel heard.' Making sure you're keeping eye contact and positioning your body towards your partner when they are speaking will also indicate that you are really listening. These little and easy adjustments can prevent possible fights from happening down the road.

It's important that during any fight, character assassinations and insults be avoided at all costs. Once it reaches the point where there's name-calling and things like that, the discussion should immediately stop. Couples are allowed to come back to the conversation when both have completely cooled down.

- Identify When It's Okay to Go to Bed Angry.

You've possibly heard that you should never go to bed angry, but there are times when you may need to sleep on the issue. If you or your partner is exhausted, you could say, 'I love you, let's talk about it in the morning.' By then, hopefully, the intensity will have vanished, and one of you probably will realize you were just tired or feeling sensitive at that particular moment. You have to evaluate the situation if you're too exhausted to resolve the fight, stop it immediately before it goes downhill fast, but make sure to deal with it within two days before you get so busy in your life again. Since if you just 'move on' but aren't emotionally connected, the next argument that occurs will most probably include *this particular* fight as well, and it'll be too overwhelming to cope with.

- Learn the Right Way to Apologize

Mature people know that apologizing is not a weakness; rather, it's a strength. By being the first to apologize, you demonstrate that you are mature, that you don't need to win the argument, and that you are willing to resolve the conflict. Apologizing is the first step towards resolving conflicts. In the following section, we'll cover this topic because as people have different love languages, they have different languages of apology as well. Recognizing that you've hurt your loved one and you owe them an apology is NOT enough. You have to know them enough to tailor your apology to their needs. It's a skill that takes practice and patience, but the results are mind-blowing once you learn it.

How To Apologize To Your Partner

Everyone makes mistakes or, in other words, 'to err is human,' but when you've vexed your partner, knowing the right way of apologizing makes all the difference. True apologies strengthen, not diminish, your relationship. Apologizing to your partner and your relationship means more than only saying, 'I'm sorry.' Here's what you can do to effectively start reconnecting again after vexing your partner:

- Demonstrate Your Sincere Apology

I know this may sound obvious to you, but we need to know what an honest apology means. A genuine apology is directed towards how you've hurt your partner and healing the damage your actions have caused, not necessarily on obtaining forgiveness. If your main goal of saying sorry is to get things back to normal in the blink of an eye and enjoy your relationship again, then your apology is not sincere and could even worsen the situation. The chances are high that your partner will realize that your apology is manipulative; you will get frustrated quickly, and things will go wrong again, and you'll end up damaging your relationship even further.

So, before you apologize, get honest with yourself about why you want to apologize. What are you genuinely sorry for? Try to see things from your partner's perspective.

- Acknowledge Your Partner's Hurt

When you feel it's time to go to your partner and sincerely apologize, prepare to get uncomfortable. Your partner may interrupt your apology by explaining how much you've hurt them and what they are going through because of your actions. In this case, it's fundamental to let them speak and not interrupt them with your opinions about the situation. *'Don't listen to respond, listen to understand.'* Apologizing can feel scary for some of us because it puts us in a vulnerable position. Naturally, following the need to protect ourselves from guilt, we get defensive. However, for the offended partner, defending your behavior and giving explanations is considered trying to get excused from the situation and avoid taking responsibility for your actions.

'Never ruin an apology with an excuse.' When someone is hurt, all they need is to feel understood. You need to genuinely demonstrate to your partner that you are aware of the pain you caused and address it directly in your apology. Take responsibility for insensitive and hurtful things you said or did. This means that you will not accuse your partner of how they've behaved and that you will resist the impulse to get defensive. Don't you ever devalue their feelings or

question the logic behind their words. Remember this, your job here is *not* to be right but to help your partner feel heard and cared for.

- Make a Plan for Change

Tell your partner what you've learned from the incident and make a list of the things that you will do or change to avoid similar mistakes in the future. However, it's important to believe in this, for false promises without fulfillment will only ruin your relationship even more.

We all are different individuals with unique traits and different needs. Thus, what you think is helpful, may not be what your partner actually needs to feel better. Instead, find out what your partner wants to find a resolution. It demonstrates to your partner that you respect them and that their feelings are valid and important to you. However, sometimes even the one who has been hurt has no idea what remedy would make things better or right. But that's okay. Providing that you show them that you are there for them, and you might not know how to make things better, but you are willing to learn, it's already heartwarming and promising.

- Don't Force Forgiveness

Understandably, you can't wait to see your relationship back on track, but remember that your principal objective was not to get forgiveness and get comfortable again quickly, but to make things much easier for your partner and start developing trust and connection again. So, give your partner some space and time to process all those unpleasant emotions of anger, disappointment, hurt, frustration and all the negative feelings they might be going through now. Don't rush them through this process or accuse them of taking 'too long' to forgive you.

After the apology, remember not to act like everything is just back to normal, and nothing ever happened. Forgiveness is a process; it doesn't happen in an instant. Even if things in your relationship seem alright shortly after the apology, wounds are probably still fresh, and you must be gentle and patient with your partner. This is a great opportunity to show them your commitment. So go on and demonstrate through your actions that you are willing to invest your energy and time in making things better for your partner, yourself and, of course, the relationship.

Tips to Resolve Relationship Conflicts

Many couples I've been helping through all these years aren't interested in any sort of change; rather, they're more interested in bashing each other's heads in. The reason is that our ego competes with our ability to live harmoniously. Sometimes we just don't want to approach or even get close to the person with whom we're in disagreement. I believe this 'joy in hostility' is rooted in the animal side of human nature we seek to withhold.

Keep in mind that to improve our relationships, we have to focus on improving ourselves, not the other person, since everyone is firstly responsible for themselves. The moment we change our approach to dealing with problems, the other person will change theirs too. You can't change someone else, and beware that everything you say does surely affects the behavior of those around you. At last, I want you to ask yourself the following question: 'What do I desire more? The rewards of a useless battle or the rewards of a close and loving relationship with the person I love?

Here are some helpful tips that can help you resolve the conflicts in your relationship:

1. Be Direct!

Sometimes partners don't just let it out and clearly explain what exactly is bothering them; instead, they pick more indirect ways of expressing their discontent. One partner may talk to the other in a condescending way and use a tone that can imply underlying hostility. Other times, partners may go through sadness and anger without really knowing the reason. Partners might also simply avoid discussing an issue by quickly changing topics when the issue comes up or by beating around the bush. But, such indirect and unproductive ways of expressing anger cannot result in a real understanding of the problem because they don't give the person, who is the target of the behaviors, a clear picture of the situation. They know that their loved one is irritated, but the lack of directness leaves them without a hint about what action to take and what words to use to resolve the conflict.

2. Find the Real Issue

Normally, arguments occur when one partner's wants are not met. If your partner is needy, maybe they feel insecure and need your support, attention or encouragement. If you're angry that your partner isn't taking out the trash, maybe you're upset because you feel like you are doing all the housework. Learn to point to the real issue so you can avoid constant fighting.

3. Practice Assertive Communication

One efficient conflict resolution strategy is to put things based on how you feel, rather than what you think the other person is doing wrong, using 'I feel' statements.

Statements that directly attack your partner's personality can be especially destructive to the relationship. *'I statements'* focus on how *you* feel, without accusing your partner, and *behavior descriptions* focus on a particular behavior your partner is engaging in, rather than a character flaw. For example, a man might say, 'I get irritated when you claim I'm flirting with someone during an innocent conversation.' These tactics are obviously direct but don't assault your partner's character.

Nevertheless, it must be pointed out that these direct negative tactics *can* be constructive in some situations. According to research, for couples with quite minor problems, rejecting and blaming one's partner during a discussion was associated with lower relationship satisfaction and worsened the problems. For couples with more *major problems,* a different picture came up: behaviors such as rejecting and blaming resulted in less satisfaction immediately after the discussion, *but surprisingly, in the long run*, the problems were resolved, and it led to an increase in relationship satisfaction.

4. Never Say Never (Nor "always")

When you're dealing with a problem, you should avoid making generalizations about your partner. Statements such as 'You *never* help me out with the housework' or, 'You're *always* staring at your cell phone when you come home from work" are likely to put your partner on the defensive. Stop prompting constant quarrels about how your partner could be more helpful or attentive; it will only lead your partner to start generating counter-examples of all the times they were really helpful or attentive. Again, you don't want to put your partner on the defensive. Never use *never* and *always* in negative sentences!

5. Choose Your Battles

If you want to have constructive discussions, remember to cope with one issue at a time. Some couples tend to drag multiple subjects into one single discussion, a conflicting habit called 'kitchen-sinking.' It refers to the old expression 'everything but the kitchen sink,' meaning that every possible thing is included. When you intend to solve personal problems, this is not probably the strategy you'd take with yourself. Imagine that you'd like to include physical exercise into your daily routine. You would not think that this would also be a great time to think about saving more money for retirement, organizing your wardrobe, and figuring out how to deal with an uncomfortable situation at work. You would try to deal with these issues one at a time. It sounds obvious, but in the heat of the moment, a fight about one topic can turn into a complaining session about the whole marriage or relationship. The more complaints you make, the less likely any of your issues will actually get entirely discussed and resolved.

7. Really listen to your partner

Feeling like your partner is not paying attention to you can be very frustrating. When you interrupt your partner or suppose that you know what they're thinking, you're not giving them a chance to express themselves openly. Even if you are certain that you know where your partner is coming from or know what they're going to say, you could still be wrong, and your partner will still feel like you're not listening.

You can show your partner that you're paying attention by using *active listening* techniques. When your partner speaks, paraphrase what they say — that is, rephrase it in your own words. That can prevent misunderstandings before they start. You can also *perception-check* by making sure that you're interpreting your partner's reactions correctly.

For example, "You seem irritated by that comment — Am I right?" These strategies prevent misunderstandings and show your partner that you're paying attention to them and care about what they're saying.

8. Don't automatically object to your partner's complaints

When you're criticized, it's hard not to get defensive. But defensiveness doesn't solve problems. Imagine a couple arguing because the wife wants her husband to do more chores around the house. When she suggests that he do a quick clean-up after he gets ready to leave in the morning, he says, "Yes, that would help, *but* I don't have time in the morning." When she suggests that he set aside some time on the weekend, he says, "Yes, that could be a way to schedule it in, *but* we usually have plans on weekends, and I have work to catch up on, so that won't work." This "yes-butting" behavior suggests that her ideas and views are not worthwhile. Another destructive, defensive behavior is "cross-complaining," when you respond to your partner's complaint with one of your own. For example, responding to "You don't clean up enough around the house" with "You're a neat freak." It's important to hear your partner out and consider what they're saying.

9. Take a different perspective

In addition to listening to your partner, you need to take their perspective and try to understand where they're coming from. Those who can take their partner's perspective are less likely to become angry during a conflict discussion.

Other research has shown that taking a more objective perspective can also be helpful. In one study, researchers staged a simple marital quality intervention, asking participants to write about a specific disagreement they had with their partners from the perspective of a neutral third party who wanted the best for both members of the couple. Couples who engaged in this 20-minute writing exercise three times a year maintained stable marital satisfaction levels over the year, while couples who didn't show declines in satisfaction.

10. Do not show contempt for your partner

Of all of the negative things you can do and say during a conflict, the worst may be *contempt*. According to my professional experience, contempt is the top predictor of separation and divorce. Contemptuous remarks are those that belittle your partner. This can involve sarcasm and name-calling. It can also include nonverbal behavior like rolling your eyes or smirking.

Such behavior is extremely disrespectful and implies that you're disgusted with your partner. Imagine that one partner says, "I wish you took me out more," and the other responds, "Oh yes, the most important thing is to see and be seen and overpay for tiny portions of food at some rip-off restaurant. Could you be more superficial?" Or one partner says they're too tired to clean up, and the other replies, "I'm sure you're *sooo* exhausted after a long day of chatting at the water cooler. I've been busting my butt all day, and you just get home and sprawl out on the couch, staring at your smartphone like a teenager." This kind of contempt makes it impossible to engage in a real discussion and is likely to elicit anger from your partner, rather than an attempt to solve the problem.

The Couple's Dialogue

Good communication skills may not solve every problem or resolve all issues, but it is an excellent place to make each other feel safe and heard. One of the most effective forms of communication in a love relationship is the couple's dialogue. It consists of four basic steps that can help build better communication with your loved ones today, providing both partners committed to this process. It should be done regularly to ensure effective communication between couples - this isn't reserved for when arguments have started or emotions are high - it's for the everyday scenarios and should help prevent disruption of your relationship in the long-term. The steps described help us to grow together in our relationship understanding each other's wants and needs.

1. Mirroring

Mirroring is about how to help your partner listen without distorting thoughts and feelings. This is the process of accurately reflecting back the content of a message from one partner. The most common form of mirroring is paraphrasing. A "paraphrase" is a statement in your own words of what the message your partner sent means to you. It indicates that you are willing to transcend your own thoughts and feelings for the moment and attempt to understand your partner from their point of view. Any response made before mirroring is often an "interpretation" and may contain a misunderstanding. Mirroring allows your partner to send their message again and permits you to paraphrase until you do understand. When the message has been heard accurately, you can then move on to the next step.

2. Validating

It's not enough just to listen. You must learn to pay close attention to understand your partner's truth. This is communication to the sending partner that the information being received and mirrored "makes sense." It indicates that you can see the information from your partner's point of view and accept that it has validity and that it is true for the partner. Validation is a temporary suspension or transcendence of your point of view that allows your partner's experience to have its own reality. Typical validating phrases are: "I can see what you're saying. I can understand why you are saying that." Such phrases convey to your partner that their subjective experience is not crazy, has its own logic, and is a valid way of looking at things. To validate your partner's message does not mean that you agree with their point of view or that it reflects your subjective experience. It merely recognizes the fact that in every situation, there are two points of view. Every report of any experience is an "interpretation," which is the "truth" for each person. The process of mirroring and validation affirms the other person and increases trust and closeness.

3. Empathizing

Once the feeling is expressed, it's time to empathize. The next big step in the dialoguing process is for your partner to empathize with your expressed feelings, fostering intimacy and emotional connection. It is the process of reflecting or imagining the feelings the sending partner is experiencing about the vent or the situation being reported. This deep level of communication attempts to recognize, reach into and, on some level, experience emotions for the sending partner. Empathy allows both partners to transcend, perhaps for a moment, their separateness and to experience a genuine "meeting." Such an experience has remarkable healing power. Typical phrases for empathic communication include: and "I can imagine that you might be feeling" or "I can see you are feeling," and "that makes sense."

A complete dialogue transaction may then sound as follows: "So, I understand you to be saying that if I don't look at you when you are talking to me, you think that I am uninterested in what you are saying. I can understand that. It makes sense to me, and I can imagine that you would feel rejected and angry. That must be a terrible feeling." The reciprocal exchange of this process is the couple's dialogue.

Chapter Five

Sharing Your Feelings With Your Spouse

There is an absolutely practical reason to express your sadness, anger or other emotions that you would usually hide. If you don't share, let's say, your anger with your partner, you deprive that person of the opportunity to solve the problem that had initially sparked the anger.

While all relationships must be built on love, attraction, respect, and mutual understanding, these emotions can only be kept if there is the chance of settling the issues down when they begin to go the wrong direction.

Sadness, irritation, anger, and other emotions provide an opportunity to communicate and give your partner a chance to address your issues and concerns. Intimacy becomes impossible if you live in fear showing all you are, including your love and feelings, needs and wants, anger and frustration, doubts, and questions. We all dislike that feeling when the other person is hiding something from us, since it indicates a lack of trust within the relationship. The simple act of suppressing anger in a relationship can cause vicious cycles of withholding, withdrawal, and further withholding, which ultimately leads to much stronger tensions and a lack of authenticity that frequently causes the relationship to fail.

Of course, it seems much easier to share your thoughts than your feelings. Sharing your deepest feelings takes emotional courage and risk because it unquestionably makes you feel exposed and vulnerable. But it is a very fundamental step to create intimacy and a strong mental connection in your marriage. Through sharing with your spouse what is in your heart, you can achieve deeper intimacy and connection.

Understanding Silence

Silence can signify many things such as: yes, no, agreement or disagreement. It can either indicate contentment or dissatisfaction, safety or fear. It may be accompanied by the smile of approval or the scorn of judgment. But the important question you want to answer is: What can the sounds of silence signify between you and your partner?

As much as there are similarities between people, and men and women tend to act in some gender predictable ways— for example, it's usually a woman saying: 'We need to talk'—couples are unique in the way they communicate. How they love, fight, speak, eat, and watch TV is, in fact, specific to them and their relationship. What silence means for two partners reflects who they are as individuals and how they relate as a couple.

Below you see some examples of experiencing silence in relationships:

- 'We can go for hours without talking and be perfectly content.'
- 'She has no thought that goes unspoken!'
- 'When things are bad, we stop talking.'
- 'He never talks.'

Misinterpretation of silence

One thing that often holds up the growth, resilience and ultimately healing of a couple is the misinterpretation of silence between them. It's not different for new partners or seasoned lovers. Couples always have an uncanny ability to feel and know what the other partner is really thinking and going through mentally, and they tend to react accordingly. Unfortunately, this often blocks expanded knowing of their partner because they fail to account for their partner's personality, induced reactions, history, and context.

- Non-Couples Issues

While there are many 'pros' to thinking as 'We,' one of the most experienced drawbacks is that you assume that all your partner's reactions, including his or her silence, are about you and your actions. The problem is that once you make that assumption, you cause yourself and your partner a great amount of confusion and anxiety.

For instance, your husband comes home after a long day at work, says hello, and then silently goes to check his emails.

Worried, you ask: 'Is everything alright?'

'Fine,' he answers.

Still worried, you ask: 'Why are you not talking to me?'

Now he sounds irritated and replies: 'I don't feel like talking right now.'

Your worries now turn into anger, and you'll say: 'I've waited for you all day to come home, and now you don't feel like talking!?'

Your partner walks into another room and leaves the situation.

Solution: Undoing this type of vicious cycle needs great team-work and trust.

To break that cycle, try the following methods:

- Let go of the Assumptions

When you ask your partner if he/she is alright and your partner replies 'fine,' just assume the best, give them the space they need, and then proceed as normal.

- Pick up the Right Clarifications

It is crucial in every relationship, whether you are an extremely close couple or a couple mending your bond, to clarify the meaning of silence throughout your relationship. When you are about to be silent for a while, you can say: 'I'm just dealing with something important at work. It's not about us'. This simple indication alleviates the situation and makes it easier for your partner to give you space.

- There is always room for options without assumptions.

It does set up a pattern of mutual understanding and respect for separate problem solving on each individual's issues. Often, when such important space-giving becomes part of a couple's relationship, the partners will not guard against it so forcefully, and they may even ask the other partner for an opinion more frequently.

- There and Then vs. Here and Now

If you find it challenging, or even impossible, not to worry or assume the worst about the silence, no matter how much your partner clarifies about it, you might be mixing your history and the people from your childhood, your primary caretakers or earlier relationships, with your current partner. Through fear, accusation and ultimately insistence, you will excessively involve the present with the past and reproduce it.

Solution: Be curious, think about the issue, write about it and try to disrupt the induced negative feelings in yourself and your partner by clarifying things for your partner, for example: 'I think I get anxious and frightened, no matter what you say, because I tend to associate silence to punishments that I received from my parents in my childhood.' After opening up and explaining the reason and history behind your feelings, however irrational they might seem, you are back in the present moment. If you seem to stick to this fear-assumption pattern, seeking help from a professional can definitely be helpful and enlightening.

- It's Just Not Me

Some particular situations shed light on the personality differences or social status of partners. For instance, when they are hanging out with other couples, she is absolutely silent, and he wants her to socialize more, or when they are having a nice evening, he likes to read the book he had been waiting to receive, but she wants him to hang out and speak with her. The differences don't necessarily imply a lack of love; they solely imply differences. The challenge here is not at all changing who you are, but working together to respect each other's style and space.

Misuse of Silence

Silent rage or the so-called silent treatment as punishment is toxic and even threatening to any relationship's spirit and vitality. Refusing to talk, despite the other partner's attempts to apologize or positively reconnect, is, in fact, an in-your-face statement that you are avoiding connection, respect and the opportunity to resolve the issues. It creates an atmosphere of confusion, fear and intimidation that makes safety, intimacy and couples' resilience difficult and even impossible.

Solution: Communicate to the silent partner through writing your feelings and your need to speak about the issues between the two of you. Suggest the use of a self-help guide or consultation with a professional. Make sure to secure your emotional and physical safety with outside resources if your partner cannot let go of his/her anger.

Positive Aspects of Silence

- Powerful Bond Between Partners:

A couple's ability to create a safe and comfortable space in silence signifies trust and peace. As many psychoanalysts described the significance of the infant's individuation process as the capacity to play on its own in the mother's presence, a couple's ability to have separate silent space while remaining connected mentally reflects their maturity, independence as well as their strong bond.

- Just Being There

When people are physically and mentally bonded, they are profoundly aware of each other's non-verbal cues. These non-verbal cues impact each partner even beyond their conscious awareness. Recognizing and utilizing "Just Being There" as a powerful recovery tool to calm and support each other in a day-to-day journey and the recovery from trauma, emphasizes the power of connection, even without words.

- What Words Can't Say

The intimate physical bond between couples cannot be put into words. For some, words cause so much misunderstanding and confusion that silent, intimate connection becomes the principal step before opening up verbally and a determining step in restoring the bond.

As a couple, consider giving new meaning to silence: through side by side meditation, sharing a walk in nature, walking side by side under the rain, driving in the "company" of the other, enjoying the sounds of silence.

When Your Partner Struggles with Expressing Emotions

When partners are not able to express their emotions, it can certainly erode the relationship. Emotions give us vital information that we can utilize to better understand our needs, priorities and limits in the present and the future. We use emotions to set boundaries and make decisions. If a partner isn't sharing their anger, sadness, loss or grief, the relationship doesn't become a safe haven for dealing with problems and conflicts.

I regularly work with couples as well as individuals who struggle with expressing their emotions. One reason behind this struggle is that individuals might have been taught that showing or even having emotions is a certain sign of weakness or not having things in control.

In scientific language, emotions are nervous system reactions to external stimuli and internal thoughts. They are not something we can control or lead towards a specific desired direction. They just show up when we do not want them to. Now take a look at this example; I may want to show how excited I am about my husband's big business event, but I'm feeling extremely overwhelmed by how much is on my plate that week. At that moment, I put on the 'good supportive wife face' and say I've never been happier in my life! I am so cheerful and proud that we are going to this event. Deep down, what is really going on, is nothing but fear, stress and a great amount of anxiety about if I could fit in another important activity that week.

My partner asks if everything's okay, and I say it can't be better! He looks at me suspiciously and asks if I'm sure. I say, 'I'm sure.' How often does this happen between couples? We only act like things are good when actually they are not. We do this to calm down our loved ones and to not disappoint them. However, in doing so, we have to push away our own feelings and ignore ourselves in some way. Think a second about what it would be like, to be honest and true to ourselves? To acknowledge how important it is to us to add that important event, and then the next step is to let our partner know about our feelings. In fact, instead of overriding our internal experience, we face it.

When someone withholds their sentiments, feeling those suppressed accumulated emotions can be scary and overwhelming. However, while emotions can be really powerful, they tend to be temporary. 'They have sort of a wave to them. They just build up, and gradually, they pass if you go through them without preventing them.'

Obviously, healthily navigating emotions is difficult, and it can be even frustrating and confusing when your partner isn't aware of their feelings and cannot communicate them. The question here is: How can you help your partner express their emotions so that this process can benefit both of you and your relationship as well?

You can consider your partner's emotions as party guests, and focus on creating a safe and supportive space for welcoming their feelings. Below you can see some useful tips.

1. Invite your partner's emotions.

'People aren't going to come over unless they're invited. You have to send out the invitation. The same theory applies to emotions, as well. It could mean creating a regular routine where you and your partner sit down and talk about emotions. If your partner does not seem ready to share their feelings at that moment, you'd better schedule a time when they completely are.

2. Adopt a non-judgmental attitude towards your partner

No one would ever be willing to attend a party where the host continuously scolds and criticizes the guests — 'What is that dress you are wearing? That's hideous! That dress is the stupidest thing I've ever seen!'

Partners need to think creatively and carefully about what kind of setting they are preparing for [their partner's] emotions. They should make sure that they accept the other partner's emotions with total respect and understanding and set an inviting, safe and comfortable place to talk and discuss this delicate issue.

An essential part of creating a welcoming and comfortable space to hear your partner's emotions is adopting a non-judgmental attitude when they finally start to express them. You should avoid saying statements such as 'How could you even be angry about that?! That doesn't make any sense' or something like: 'You should not feel that way, that issue is so petty and trivial! '. Keep in mind that judging your partner's emotions will only make them more defensive and ultimately distant from you.

3. Pay careful attention to your own reactions

As for judging your partner's emotions, your reactions, even the smallest ones, can potentially block the conversation from happening. If you find out that you are becoming defensive, upset, or angry, acknowledging those emotions can substantially help your partner.

For instance, you might say something like: 'I know I speak with that nervous tone when I start speaking about my job. Let me know please when you feel like I'm using that tone'.

There are other times when both of you need a timeout.

If you struggle with your emotions too, you should keep in mind that having and experiencing emotions is certainly not a weakness or something to control. Instead, emotions provide us with valuable information about ourselves, our partner and the world around us.

Instead of ignoring your emotions or blaming yourself for experiencing them, try to discover how your emotions have helped you for your own good in the past. Start journaling about emotional topics or your significant life events, even for a short time. This helps you process your emotions. And then if you feel safe, you can share the emotion with someone else, he said.

The Right Way to Express Feelings

We are humans, and it's only natural for humans to have feelings. If we express our feelings in unpleasant ways, it will naturally trigger disconnect and detachment in our relationships. On the other hand, safely expressing feelings can definitely lead to a stronger connection between partners. Knowing how to express feelings tactfully is essential if you want to build trust, be the closest person to your partner, and, most importantly, sustain your relationships in a healthy way.

Sharing positive feelings can certainly solidify relationships. Love, appreciation, gratitude, delight—sharing these feelings builds strong and affectionate connections.

At the same time, stress, anxiety, and overall ups and downs occur in everyone's life, leaving us scared, sad or angry. Also, differences and hurt feelings will come over every now and then, between just any two people who interact regularly. Sharing feelings enables you to analyze the situation that had caused the problem. That way, you will figure out how the difficulty happened in the first place, and you'll decide what actions to take to fix it. One interesting thing about problem-solving together is that it can make negative feelings go away, make the relationship sweeter and ultimately build a stronger bond between you and your partner.

What Characteristics Does a Constructive Way of Expressing Feelings Have?

Often, when we start to talk about a feeling, we go with these two simple words: '*I feel...*' Then, we continue with a 'feeling word,' that is, a state such as upset, disappointed, delighted, tired or confused, etc. If you find yourself having difficulty identifying the feeling, you can try multiple choices; that is, you will have to pick from these four basic feelings: sad, glad, mad or scared.

The mistake that people often make when trying to share a feeling is saying: *'I feel that...'* The word *that* makes it look like the sentence will be about a thought, not a feeling.

It's fine to share a thought, but thoughts give us dry information, not the real essence of what you are truly experiencing within. Feelings, surprisingly, have a stronger impact on our connections. So, while sharing your thoughts builds a sense of bonding, the connection is much less intense than when you also look within yourself and share the feelings you discover there: discouraged, hopeless, pleased, weary, frustrated, positive, delighted, dejected, etc.

What Is the Most Common Mistake Then?

Too often, instead of beginning with 'I feel...' people start with the phrase, *'You make me feel...'*, which can trigger some trouble.

'You make me feel...' is one of those phrases that I hear my patients saying far too often —not because I work with bad people, but because most people are not aware that, **"You make me feel..."** can hurt others' feelings and cause arguments.

But why does the phrase 'You make me feel ...' consistently leads to a defective start? Here are five main reasons why—and why replacing it with 'I feel...' is much wiser and more efficient.

- 'You make me feel...'. This start sounds like an accusation or a statement of blame, not a statement about your inner feelings.

Statements about feelings, especially about those vulnerable feelings like sad, confused, or anxious, often inspire empathy from most listeners. Accusations, on the other hand, are off-putting, stimulating antagonism and defensiveness.

Now, try to compare the following groups of phrases. Which group would you prefer to hear from your partner?

Group A:

- I feel sad.
- I feel uncomfortable.
- I feel stupid.

Group B:

- You make me sad.
- You make me feel uncomfortable.
- You make me feel stupid.

Can you feel the difference? If not, read them again, this time slowly and aloud.

- The sentence starting with 'You make me feel...' is disempowering.

By starting with 'You make me feel...', you give away your power to fix your negative feelings. The phrase turns you into a helpless victim. While the phrase may potentially induce shame or guilt in your partner, it simultaneously makes you or at least make you seem impotent and passive.

On the contrary, beginning with 'I feel...' gives you, not the other person, the power to understand what really makes you feel better. Maybe your negative feelings result from being hungry, tired, or overloaded, or you've been going through a challenging situation that needs considerable mental energy to figure out how to proceed with it.

Therefore, when stating your feelings, it's recommended that you start with the pronoun 'I' and the phrase 'I feel…', since it is empowering, making both you and your partner focus on your issue. Now, together, you can delve into finding possible solutions.

- You make me feel … stimulates counter-accusations.

As I mentioned previously, the phrase 'You make me feel…' sounds like an attack in some ways, and an attack brings about counter-attacks. Using this phrase at the beginning of sharing your feelings, you lead your conversation into a heated argument.

Let's have a look at the example below together:

Sophie: You make me feel so unattractive lately. You barely ever compliment me. It's so disappointing.

Jake: Well, maybe that's because you make me feel like an awful husband!

As you observed, as simple as that, this couple is off down the road of fighting. When Jake hears that Sophie started with 'You make me feel,' he gets defensive and totally tunes out from listening to her concerns, and what was supposed to be a helpful conversation turns into a ridiculous quarrel.

On the other hand, when another couple, Anna and James, face the same situation with a different approach, which is beginning with 'I feel…', the dialogue, surprisingly, turns out to be quite productive.

Anna: I feel so unattractive lately. When you barely ever compliment me, I think that I never look good to you.

James: I'm so sorry, honey, you feel that way. In fact, I just adore how you look. I probably could tell you more often about how much I appreciate your looks and especially your charming smile. I definitely must admit that lately I've been so busy with work that I haven't noticed much else.

Anna: It's so heart-warming that we are actually talking about this. I feel better already, you see, just understanding more about what's going on with your job calmed me down. You know what? I also wonder why I suddenly had this upsurge of needing compliments. Maybe it's because I have been feeling somehow abandoned seeing you spending so much time working.

By launching with the words "I feel..." Anna inspires empathy in James and shares problem-solving instead of provoking counter-accusations.

- The phrase 'You make me feel...' is grounded on a misunderstanding

In general, one person does not, by themselves, make another feel anything. Here, the most significant point to note is paying attention to the whole combination of what one partner says or does and the other partner's *interpretation* of those words or actions.

For example, you try to make me laugh, and I may respond with mild amusement, but I may also respond with annoyance, scorn, frustration, or with great appreciation and laughing hard. It's the combination of what you say and do and what *I* bring to the context that determines the situation. That is, a listener's response comes not only from factors within the listener but also from what the other person has said/done.

- 'You make me feel...' focuses on your partner and takes the focus away from YOU.

'You make me feel...', followed by a negative word, sets you into a stance of criticism towards your partner. 'I feel...', by contrast, launches an exploration of what you are feeling and why you are feeling that way particularly. That's a path to self-discovery.

Look at this example: 'I feel abandoned when you bring home too much work in the evenings, leaving me all by myself. I was thinking to myself that maybe I need to discover something to enjoy evenings on my own instead of continuously wanting your attention. I used to enjoy reading novels a lot—maybe I should start again'.

How to Talk About Feelings with Your Partner

How you express your feelings determines how receptively your feelings will be heard. At the same time, the person you are sharing your feelings with has a major role in whether the discussion will be productive or not. For instance, selfish people may experience irritation when their partner shares his/her vulnerable feelings, no matter how that feeling has been expressed. Others may even go further and take those negative feelings you describe personally, considering it as criticism towards themselves.

Sharing your feelings in a relationship is crucial to developing respect, understanding, safety and, most importantly, mutual trust.

- Get in touch with your own emotions

The first step towards getting more comfortable with your own emotions, and finally being able to express them to your partner in a productive way, is to spend sufficient time getting familiar with your emotions and figuring them out. One excellent way to do this is journaling, which countless psychologists recommend. It not only makes you feel liberated and sets you free from that negativity inside, but also gives you a whole new outlook regarding your emotions in general. Often, identifying and showing your vulnerable side to your partner and telling them how you are feeling is difficult. That's because we can't identify our feelings and process them ourselves in the first place. How can you expect to be able to explain to your partner about how you feel when you don't know what's going on inside you yet, right?

Therefore, if you want to build a strong connection and, consequently, a stable relationship with your partner, you must have a strong and deep relationship with yourself first!

- Calm down before talking

Avoid responding immediately to emotional triggers. In the heat of the moment, you may say things that you'd regret afterward, because you may not be rational at that moment. So, try to take some time before reacting to your emotional trigger. Some people set a 48-hour-rule for themselves. Others need less time to recover their emotional balance. Some people choose to write down everything they want to say and then later pick those things that really make sense.

- Try to use 'I feel' statements.

If you're working on being open and comfortable with your feelings, using more 'I feel' statements is a great way to start. One of the biggest reasons why we refuse to express our feelings, especially if those feelings are harmful because of something going on in the relationship, is that we are afraid that our words will upset or irritate our partner. To keep this from happening, try to make a distinction between the behavior affecting your feelings rather and the person causing it. By doing so, you will reduce that feeling of guilt or blaming yourself and increases focus on the emotions.

- Create an atmosphere for mutual understanding

If you need to emphasize your partner's role in your feelings, start your sentences with 'When you...'. For example, 'When you came home so late last night from work, I felt extremely lonely.' Continue then with, "My concern was…" At this point, you are on the road to mutual understanding.

- Focus on deeper issues.

If you're struggling to open up about your feelings, take the time to get to the root of how you are really feeling and then have a conversation with your partner about it. Often when we are angry, there is something deeper going on that we are simply masking with anger. It may be sadness, fear or even some unresolved issues in your past, which are not addressed so far and deserve some work and dedication.

Overall, identifying that deeper emotion that is going on helps us to develop a deeper connection; in other words, rather than staying in a reactive mode, we transition to a reflective mode.

- Keep in mind that being open works wonders for both of you in the relationship.

It's not easy to show your vulnerable side; that's why being able to show it is a precious gift you give not just to yourself but also to your partner and, in consequence, your relationship. Being open about your feelings gives your partner something they need: certainty. Because at the end of the day, all of us need to be reminded that we're enough and that we're loved and special. When two partners are what I call 'emotionally naked,' they give each other the precious gift of certainty that they will be loved, respected and safe, which leads to the development of a stronger connection.

Ultimately, here, the main takeaway is that you don't have to know precisely how to open up regarding your feelings right now; actually, it's all about the process and dedicating enough energy and effort. Over time, everything will go smoothly, but congratulations! I want to let you know that even just wanting to take the first step, and the fact that you are willing to work on is a great start on its own!

Tips to Enhance Effective Emotional Communication

When we talk about *Emotional Communication,* we mean when a couple creates relationship-relevant meaning to maintain their connection. This could be listening to your special, memorable song, giving a kind smile, sharing a laugh, buying a small sweet gift, touching in respectful and caring ways or helping your partner in small, meaningful ways. All these are relevant for them as a unique couple. This type of communication is the life-blood of a relationship. It allows shared meaning and emotion to flow and grow between the partners. It cracks the code for emotionally healthy relationships. Paying attention to each other's ways of trying to connect is the most important thing to take note of.

The interesting point is that communication does not always necessarily be deep, meaningful and significant. You don't even have to agree with each other. The most important thing is *how* you pay attention to each other. Here are ten principal ways to encourage effective emotional communication in your relationship:

- Create an emotional connection with your partner

Take a moment to look into their eyes, hold their hands, and try to remember and re-experience the reasons why you fell in love with them in the first place.

- Create an atmosphere of openness; encourage your partner to talk with you

Start with asking fun questions, such as 'What do you think has been the best destination we've traveled to so far? Remembering fun things is a great way to start a conversation. Once the door is open, taking the conversation to the next level is quite trouble-free.

- Assure your partner that it is definitely safe to talk about emotions

Let your partner know you are there for them. It can be utterly empowering to say: 'You can cry on my shoulder if you ever need to, and I won't ever think you're feeble; your feelings are valid, important and legitimate.' Once your partner is assured that they will not be judged for showing their emotional and vulnerable side, they will be more willing to share their deeper feelings.

- Help each other to learn basic conflict resolution skills

In every conversation, no matter how heated, there is a speaker and a listener. When the speaker is speaking, the listener must hear what they are saying. Then the roles reverse. This alone will make difficult conversations much easier.

- Encourage informality—learn to be relaxed around each other

If things get complicated, and you need to walk on eggshells, tell your partner that you feel the tension as well and that you are willing to drop the attitude.

- Encourage your partner to bring their 'whole' to the relationship

Let them know that they don't have to modify their feelings or change themselves. Assure your partner that you are a hundred percent willing to hear all that there is.

- Tell your partner that as a human, you can make mistakes

As William Arthur Ward puts it well, 'To make mistakes is human and to stumble is commonplace.' All of us make mistakes; however, we must remember that there's always a possibility to compromise and fix things for the better.

- Support your partner with thinking out loud

Not only words speak. Even if people don't speak their minds, their behaviors will reveal what's really going on. Talking about your negative feelings will prevent you from acting upon them, and perhaps from creating an unnecessary fight.

- Stick to the belief that laughter is good, but playing it 'cool' is not

A sense of humor is probably one of the greatest qualities you can own and use in a relationship. Couples with a sense of humor laugh together more and tend to stay together longer. Being able to joke about your lives is a good sign that things are healing.

- Your strong emotional connection to your partner makes the impossible seem possible

Developing a strong emotional bond will help both of you to handle the inevitable hardships that arise in life more smoothly. Using these tips, you will add to the depth of your communication and your relationship. Couples who trust each other enough to share their true feelings build wonderful relationships.

Chapter Six

Validating Emotions and Feelings

Acceptance is one of the four options we have in each problem circumstance. One way of communicating acceptance of ourselves and others is through validation. Validation is a technique of supporting and deepening a relationship while keeping a different point of view when your best friend or family member makes a decision you don't think is wise. Even when you differ on issues, validation shows that the relationship is dynamic and vital.

Acknowledging and accepting another person's thoughts, feelings, sensations, and behaviors as understandable is known as validation. Identifying and accepting your thoughts, feelings, experiences, and behaviors as understandable is self-validation.

Six levels of validation

It takes practice to learn how to apply validation properly. It will be beneficial to understand the so-called six stages of validation.

#1- Being present is the initial level. There are numerous approaches to being present. Being present can include things like holding someone's hand during a painful medical procedure, listening intently and doing nothing but listening to a child describing their day in first grade, and going to a friend's house at midnight to sit with them while they cry because they're going through a painful breakup.

Multitasking while listening to your teenager's soccer game story is not being present, and being present entails focusing your full attention on the person you're validating.

Being present for yourself entails acknowledging and sitting with your own experience rather than "running away," avoiding, or pushing it away. It's not easy to sit with so many different emotions going on; I'm aware of the fact that even joy or excitement might make you feel uneasy at times.

Other individuals are frequently uncomfortable with intense emotions since they don't know what to say. Often, the answer is simply being there and paying nonjudgmental attention to the person. Being aware of your own emotions is the first step toward accepting your feelings.

#2 - Accurate reflection is the second stage of validation. Accurate reflection entails synthesizing what you've heard from others or synthesizing your feelings. Others can do this in an awkward, sing-songy, phony, extremely aggravating style, or you can critically do it yourself. Accurate reflection is affirming when done authentically to truly comprehend the experience rather than judge it.

This type of validation can sometimes help people sort through their thoughts and separate them from their emotions. A self-reflection might be, "So basically, I'm feeling very angry and hurt." Someone else's realistic portrayal of you could be, "Sounds like you're disappointed in yourself because you didn't call him back."

#3 - Mindreading is the third level. Mindreading entails speculating on how another person is feeling or thinking. People's capacity to recognize their own emotions varies. Some people mix up worry with excitement, and others mix up happiness and excitement. Some people may not express themselves clearly because they could not experience their emotions or learn to be fearful of them.

People may hide their sentiments because they've learned that others don't like their sensitivity. This masking might result in not acknowledging even their own feelings to themselves. Therefore, it's crucial to be able to appropriately name feelings in order to acknowledge them.

Take note of how someone feels when they describe a problem to you. Then, help them label their feelings or make an educated guess about how they feel.

Level Three validation is "I'm guessing her comment must have quite wounded you." Keep in mind that you could make a mistake, and the person could correct you. It's their emotion, and they are the only one who truly understands what they're going through. Accepting their reprimand is reassuring.

#4 - Understanding the person's conduct in terms of their history and biology is the fourth level. Your experiences and biology influence your emotional reactions. Your closest friend is unlikely to appreciate playing with your German Shepherd if she was attacked by a dog a few years ago. "Given what happened to you, I entirely understand your aversion to being around my dog," says validation at this level. Understanding your own reactions in the light of your past experiences is self-validation.

#5 - Normalizing or identifying emotions is level five. Everyone benefits from knowing that their emotions are expected, and knowing that anyone would be disturbed in a particular situation validates the emotionally sensitive individual. As an example, "Obviously, you're worried. Anyone who gets nervous about speaking in front of an audience for the first time should avoid doing so."

#6 - The sixth level is radical authenticity. When you understand a person's emotion on a deep level, you have demonstrated radical authenticity. Maybe you've experienced something similar, and sharing that experience is radical authenticity.

It may sound simple to comprehend the levels, but it's generally more difficult to put them into practice. Making validation a natural aspect of your communication requires practice.

Consider the following scenario. Your best friend is unhappy because her spouse chopped up her credit card. He's treating her like a child, and he's so controlling that she can't breathe. When you question her why he didn't pay the bill, she says she overspent for the fourth time, pushing the balance over the limit by buying expensive shoes, and they couldn't afford to pay it. How can you prove your point to her? Remember to set the level to the highest possible. Before you continue reading, consider your answer!

The highest level you could possibly use is probably Level 2. "I understand, your husband chopped up your credit card without your permission—that made you feel like he was acting like a parent," you could add. You mirror her ideas and emotions back to her, demonstrating that you accept her feelings as authentic and as her own.

You probably wouldn't be able to employ Level 6 or radical authenticity because you may have had similar experiences to hers, such as going through the same thing Level 5 would not work because most people would agree that his response was logical and that they would not be outraged in that situation. Nothing in her history would make her response more understandable, so Level 4 is not an option. Level 3 is also inapplicable because she has stated her views unequivocally—there is no need to guess.

Let's look at another scenario. Jesse informs you that she has resigned from her position. She resigned after her employer publicly chastised her in front of others. She's urged him twice to not embarrass her, but he's prone to losing his cool. She was terrified of him since he reminded her of a verbally abusive uncle, and she couldn't work for him any longer. What is the level of validation that you would employ here?

In this case, Level 6 or Level 5 might be appropriate. You might affirm her feelings by expressing, "I've been in a similar position, or I truly get how she felt." "I understand totally, and I would have acted in the same way." That's the sixth level. "I believe most people would have felt the same way you did," says Level 5.

Despite her history of verbal abuse, you don't utilize Level 4 since Level 5 is appropriate. Always utilize the greatest possible level. "Given your history of being verbally attacked, I understand why you might resign," says Level 4. That's ineffective because everyone, whether they've been verbally abused before or not, would be offended if their supervisor degraded them.

Joanna gives you a call and tells you about her diet. She laments that she has overeaten chocolate cake and wants to eat more but is afraid of gaining weight. What level of validation do you have access to?

Level 3 is an excellent option. Joanna did not mention her emotions, even though she was eating for emotional reasons. You might say, "Is there something going on? I'm guessing you're irritated about something." Then she informs you that her six-year-old cat died yesterday. You could utilize a Level 5 or 6 at that point, depending on how you feel about losing a pet.

Shawna nearly drowned in a vast pond when she was a teenager. She swam out further than she realized because she was a bad swimmer. Her feet couldn't touch the bottom when she stopped swimming, so she gulped water. She became distressed, and a friend swam to her rescue. She's been frightened of water ever since. She was asked to a pool party by a friend. Even though she was just in waist-high water, she panicked when a guy who was flirting with her pulled her into the pool. She tells you she's embarrassed by her reaction and is afraid of being considered insane by the people at the party.

In this case, Level 4 validation would work. "You panicked when you were shoved into the water; given your past experience of almost drowning, anyone would probably have the same reaction."

Emotional invalidation

When a person's thoughts and feelings are rejected, ignored, or judged, this is known as emotional invalidation. Invalidation is painful for everyone, but it is more painful for someone who is emotionally sensitive.

Invalidation causes emotional distance and ruins relationships. When people invalidate themselves, they generate a sense of alienation, making it difficult to develop an identity.

Recovery from depression and anxiety is made more difficult by self-invalidation and invalidation by others. Some people believe that invalidation is a key cause of emotional problems.

Most people would argue that they do not invalidate other people's internal experiences, and few would deliberately invalidate someone else. However, well-intentioned individuals may be uncomfortable with strong emotions or mistakenly assume they are helping when they are actually invalidating.

Many people would agree that they invalidate themselves but would argue that they deserve it. They may argue that they are unworthy of appreciation and praise. Validation isn't the same as self-acceptance; it's simply acknowledging that an internal or psychological experience occurred.

Verbal Invalidation

People who care about you can invalidate you for various reasons and in a variety of ways. Here are a few examples.

Misunderstanding what it means to be close: Some people believe that knowing exactly how another person feels without asking them shows they are emotionally close to them. It's as if they know you so well as you know yourself, so they don't ask questions and may even tell you what you're thinking and feeling.

Misunderstanding of the term "validation": Some people invalidate because they feel that they agree by validating. Someone can disagree with you if you say, "You think it's wrong that you're angry with your friend." Validation is not the same as agreement. However, to soothe you, they invalidate your thoughts by saying, "You shouldn't think that way."

Trying to make your feelings better: "Don't be sad, please. Do you fancy some ice cream?" People who care about you don't want you to be sad; therefore, they may dismiss your thoughts and feelings to make you feel better.

Not wanting to harm your feelings: People will sometimes lie to you to avoid hurting your feelings. Perhaps they tell you that you look wonderful in a dress that isn't the most flattering. Perhaps they agree with your point of view in a debate, but they do not believe you are being reasonable.

Wishing the best for you: Those who care about you wish the best for you. As a result, they may do things for you that you could perform yourself. Or they push you to make friends with someone influential even if you don't like them, telling you that they're a terrific friend when that isn't the case for you. "She's someone you should be friends with, and she'll be a great companion for you."

Invalidation can be done in a variety of methods. I've included a couple of examples below.

Blaming: "You have to always be the crybaby, always upset about something, and ruin every holiday," she says. "Why didn't you fill-up the car with gas before coming home? You never think and always make things more difficult." But remember that blaming is usually a waste of time. (Taking responsibility is not the same as blaming.)

Hoovering: When you try to vacuum up any unpleasant feelings or avoid giving honest responses because you don't want to upset or be vulnerable, you're hoovering. When something is significant to you, saying "it's not such a big deal" is hoovering. Hoovering is when you say someone did an excellent job when they didn't or that your friends loved them when they didn't. Hoovering is when you don't acknowledge how difficult something is for you. When you're overwhelmed, saying, "No problem, of course, I can accomplish it" is hoovering.

Judgment: "You are overreacting" and "That is a silly concept" are examples of judging invalidation. "Here we go again, crying over nothing, letting those enormous tears pour because the grass is growing," mockery says.

Denying: "You are not angry, I know how you act when you're angry," or "You have eaten so much, I know you're not hungry" both invalidate the other person by implying that they don't feel what they say they feel.

Minimizing: "Don't worry, it's nothing, and you'll simply be up all night worrying about nothing" is usually said with the best of intentions. The message remains the same: don't feel what you're feeling.

Nonverbal Invalidation

Rolling the eyes and drumming the fingers agitatedly are examples of nonverbal invalidation. It is invalidating if someone constantly checks their phone while speaking with them. Attending an important meeting with a colleague while only paying attention to your emails or playing a game on your smartphone invalidates whether that is the message the person intended to send or not.

Working too much, purchasing too much, or overall not paying attention to your feelings, thoughts, needs, and goals are all nonverbal forms of self-invalidation.

How to be more validating

How can a person control their emotions if they believe their feelings are incorrect? This pessimistic viewpoint might lead to depression or anxiety. Validating one's emotions and sentiments, on the other hand, might help one develop a sense of self and identity. Understanding emotions can help a person better regulate their emotions.

Self-validation is the first step. To deal with this, you need to be aware of both your internal experience and your actions and behaviors. People frequently fight their feelings by criticizing themselves for how they react to situations and occurrences. Sometimes a person wants to ignore how they feel on the inside by somehow numbing themselves by using drugs or other self-destructive behaviors.

Validation helps in the identification of your feelings. Because recognizing what you're experiencing can be difficult, you might want to consider what caused the emotion in the first place. It's also crucial to be kind to yourself; people are usually quick to dismiss their emotions and engage in self-criticism.

Validation is the most effective technique to avoid invalidating others or yourself. It's never about lying, and it's about respecting the validity and understandability of another person's internal experience, and that's a powerful statement.

Conclusion

Throughout this book, we primarily emphasized the important role communication plays in relationships. We also discussed how to avoid the most common communication mistakes that can ruin our happiness. Then, we argued about solutions in detail, meticulously analyzing the most effective techniques to improve our ability to communicate, manage and resolve conflicts between couples, and share our feelings, experiences, and emotions with our partner openly and honestly.

Relationships are a very influential part of our lives; however, it's not always easy to keep open communication channels within them. Life gets hectic, and it creeps up between our partners and us in more diverse ways. Part of bridging that gap is learning well how to talk and share with one another in healthy and productive ways every day. The power of an effective communicator can actually be owned by any one of us. It empowers us to bond with our partner on a deeper level, and it is the tool by which we present ourselves. It's crucial for every relationship to survive, and it takes time and practice to develop. Only when we understand communication in our relationships we can start to figure out the techniques that let us unlock our love in brand new ways. By now, you know that good communication is vital, and it has several impressive benefits that can help us to grow both inside and out as partners and human beings.

When we open up to our partners, we allow them to see us as we truly are, and we can fully observe ourselves and see things as they really are. Effective communication is a powerful tool that will help us solve almost any hardship in our relationships when we know how to utilize it.

Share your experiences, and don't simply hold onto ordinary questions as a means of 'connecting.' Tell your partner about yourself in an honest and open way, and prove yourself to deserve their trust so that they can open up about their own experiences. Try to use small talk as a tool to warm up the situation and investigate the pathways of mutual bonding. Connecting with our partner on a deeper level takes time and energy, and it is a nuanced process. Let it unfold naturally by increasing the number of little experiences you share down the road. When in doubt, be brave and ask more questions, be as hungry to know about your significant other as you are to talk about yourself. When you actively listen and invest in the other person in the relationship, you inspire and encourage them to follow your path.

Relationships are challenging, but they're also rewarding when they're healthy and balanced. Part of reaching that balance requires learning how to communicate more effectively. Committing to making things a little better every single day, we can discover the secrets of our partner's hearts and, in the process, discover our own too. Good relationships can be developed from the rubble, but we have to commit to the journey each and every day.

Last but not least, make your relationship stronger today by sticking to communication like never before. Remember that good things don't come easy! You have to work for it.

Good Luck then!

www.ingramcontent.com/pod-product-compliance
Lightning Source LLC
Chambersburg PA
CBHW071517080526
44588CB00011B/1454